Introduction to

SYSTEMS COST-EFFECTIVENESS

PUBLICATIONS IN OPERATIONS RESEARCH

Operations Research Society of America

Editor for Publications in Operations Research
DAVID B. HERTZ

No. 1. QUEUES, INVENTORIES AND MAINTENANCE
Philip M. Morse

No. 2. FINITE QUEUING TABLES
L. G. Peck and R. N. Hazelwood

No. 3. EFFICIENCY IN GOVERNMENT THROUGH SYSTEMS ANALYSIS
Roland N. McKean

No. 4. A COMPREHENSIVE BIBLIOGRAPHY ON OPERATIONS RESEARCH*
Operations Research Group, Case Institute

No. 5. PROGRESS IN OPERATIONS RESEARCH, VOLUME I
Edited by Russell L. Ackoff

No. 6. STATISTICAL MANAGEMENT OF INVENTORY SYSTEMS*
Harvey M. Wagner

No. 7. PRICE, OUTPUT, AND INVENTORY POLICY*
Edwin S. Mills

No. 8. A COMPREHENSIVE BIBLIOGRAPHY ON OPERATIONS RESEARCH, 1957–1958*
Operations Research Group, Case Institute

No. 9. PROGRESS IN OPERATIONS RESEARCH, VOLUME II
David B. Hertz and Roger T. Eddison

No. 10. DECISION AND VALUE THEORY
Peter C. Fishburn

No. 11. HANDBOOK OF THE POISSON DISTRIBUTION
Frank A. Haight

No. 12. OPERATIONS RESEARCH IN SELLER'S COMPETITION: A STOCHASTIC MICROTHEORY
S. Sankar Sengupta

No. 13. BAYESIAN DECISION PROBLEMS & MARKOV CHAINS
J. J. Martin

No. 14. MATHEMATICAL MODELS OF ARMS CONTROL AND DISARMAMENT: APPLICATION OF MATHEMATICAL STRUCTURES IN POLITICS
Thomas L. Saaty

No. 15. FOURTH INTERNATIONAL CONFERENCE ON OPERATIONS RESEARCH
David B. Hertz and Jacques Melese

No. 16. PROGRESS IN OPERATIONS RESEARCH VOLUME III
RELATIONSHIP BETWEEN OPERATIONS RESEARCH AND THE COMPUTER
J. S. Aronofsky

No. 17. INTRODUCTION TO SYSTEMS COST EFFECTIVENESS
Karl Seiler, III

* Out-of-print

Introduction to SYSTEMS COST-EFFECTIVENESS

KARL SEILER, III

WILEY-INTERSCIENCE
A Division of John Wiley and Sons
New York · London · Sydney · Toronto

10 9 8 7 6 5 4 3 2 1

Library of Congress Catalog Card Number: 78-76062
SBN 471 77555 X

Printed in the United States of America

To Mary Louise, Abigail, Butch,
and Mary Beth

PREFACE

It may be said that the Department of Defense, under the leadership of former Secretary Robert S. McNamara and his assistant, Charles J. Hitch, has been the focal point of the development of the cost-effectiveness approach to systems planning. Notwithstanding the fact that the cost-effectiveness approach has been successfully applied within the military establishment, one should distinguish between these contributions to better management and other aspects of the McNamara regime that have come under criticism. The reason for making the distinction is to avoid condemning the cost-effectiveness discipline merely because it has been spawned in an environment in which many other decision criteria are inevitably involved, some of which have naturally been open to question, particularly with respect to Vietnam. Likewise the cost-effectiveness discipline should not be condemned merely because it is not an exact science and therefore is not infallible. It can only claim to reduce the margin of error, not eliminate it. Errors have been made with the cost-effectiveness approach and can be expected to continue to be made, but hopefully their frequency of occurrence and their magnitude will both diminish with further experience.

As a result of its many accomplishments within the military establishment, the cost-effectiveness approach today is spreading to many other parts of government as well as throughout industry. This rapid growth, however, has left the serious student and practitioner interested in these developments to the tedious task of collecting material from many sources in order to get an integrated understanding of the subject. Until now it has not been possible to obtain a concise yet comprehensive textbook on cost-effectiveness theory and applications.

This book is an outgrowth of lecture notes prepared for courses in systems cost-effectiveness given at the Radio Corporation of America's Defense Electronic Product Division, the Boeing Company, the Lockheed Corporation, and various professional societies. In the absence of a suitable text it was found desirable to provide these people with an extensive set of notes as an alternative to independent research. Their background was mainly systems engineering management but included marketing and administrative management as well.

An important consideration in a pedagogical effort of this nature was to avoid the development of the mathematical understanding already present in the lecture audience. Accordingly, the lectures assumed a basic understanding of the calculus and probability theory. The book also assumes that the reader has this much basic background; however, it is recognized that some readers may be deficient in these subjects. It has been prepared in a manner that attempts to compensate as much as possible for the lack of background. The reader is strongly advised, nevertheless, to consult the various recommended readings in those subjects for a fuller understanding. Accordingly, no attempt is made at mathematical rigor. On the contrary, an intuitive approach, combined with brief literary explanations, is used throughout. Care has been taken to balance the exposition in a manner that will ensure the coverage of the principle subjects while relegating as much of the supporting material as possible to the numerous referenced documents.

An elaborate bibliography of all works on related subjects is not presented; rather each part is followed by a list of suggested readings for additional study. These references are highly selective and were chosen with a view to recommending well-regarded contributions on each subject, many of which are original efforts.

Since this is a condensed text, it does not consider minute details or trace the discovery of ideas. The entire effort synthesizes the work of numerous specialists, many of whom are well known for their expertise. The principal motivation has been to bring a unified, concise, and understandable body of systems-oriented cost-effectiveness methodology before the reader.

KARL SEILER, III

Cinnaminson, New Jersey
March 1, 1969

ACKNOWLEDGMENTS AND CREDITS

My colleagues, past and present, are the source and inspiration for many of the ideas expressed herein. They are, in particular, Dr. Alvin B. Glenn, Systems Engineering Manager, Radio Corporation of America's Defense Systems Division; Dr. Ellis L. Rabben, Project Manager, Institute for Defense Analyses; and Mr. Nathan Tonelson, Branch Manager, Systems Analysis Division at the Communications Satellite Corporation. I must also acknowledge my sincere gratitude to Mr. David Shore, Chief Engineer, RCA Defense Electronic Products, for his original stimulation for the lectures and to Mr. Louis B. Early, COMSAT Corporation, Manager of Engineering Economy, for providing me with added encouragement to complete the book. To the students who served as guinea pigs for the assimilation of the original lecture material, I owe much for improvements made throughout.

I am also much indebted to Dr. David B. Hertz and his ORSA editorial staff for having constructively reviewed the entire manuscript.

In the preparation of the manuscript, I wish to express my sincere thanks to Mr. Curtis L. Adkins, Technical Editor, COMSAT Corporation, for reading and editing the entire manuscript and to Mmes. Frances E. Wille and Deanna J. Wallace for their competence and devotion to typing the manuscript.

Finally, I, and not any of the individuals or organizations who have helped me, am solely responsible for the development of the ideas and views expressed herein.

K. S., III

CONTENTS

INTRODUCTION 1

Suggested Readings 3

I. COST FACTORS 5

1. Level of Use 5
2. Inheritance 6
3. Research and Development 7
4. Inputs 9
5. Output 10
   Total, Variable, Fixed, Average, Marginal Costs 10
   Optimal Return Output versus Optical Efficiency Output 13
   Relative Activity Levels 14
   Short-Run, Long-Run Cost 15
6. Time 16
   Discounted Cost 17
   Obtainability Cost 18
7. Performance 19
8. Geographic Location 20
   Suggested Readings 20

II. SYSTEM COST MODELS 23

1. Matrix Model 23
2. Cost of Elements 25
3. Model Expansion 28
4. Minimizing Total System Cost 31
5. Period Costing 31
6. Time Phasing 33
7. Fixed Cost Proration 33
8. Variable Cost Nonlinearity 34
9. Cost Model Aggregation 36
10. Differential Cost Models 38
11. Probabilistic Cost 39
    Suggested Readings 43

III. SYSTEM EFFECTIVENESS MODELS 45

1. Probability Product Model 45
2. Basic Performance 47
   Confidence Limits 47
   Multiple Performance Parameters 49
3. Availability 52
4. Reliability 54
5. Survivability 56
   Microanalysis 57
   Macroanalysis 58
6. Model Expansion 59
7. Maximizing Total System Effectiveness 61
8. Period versus Mission Effectiveness 64
9. Time Phasing 66
10. Probabilistic Effectiveness 67
   Suggested Readings 68

IV. SYSTEM COST-EFFECTIVENESS MODELS 71

1. Domain of Feasibility 71
2. Homogeneity 72
   Time 72
   Geography 73
   Possession 73
   Scale 73
3. Ratio Model 74
   Optimal Efficiency System versus Optimal Effectiveness System 76
   Limitations 76
4. Indifference Curve Model 77
   Combinations of Two Systems 77
   Combinations of Three and > Three Systems 82
   Limitations 83
5. Mathematical Programming 83
6. Theory of Games 86
7. Probabilistic Cost-Effectiveness 91
8. Decision Making and the Cost-Effectiveness Criterion 96
   Technological Advances 97
   Resource Availability 97
   Political Sensitivity 98
   Psychological Stimulus 99
   Suggested Readings 101

OTHER REFERENCES 103

INDEX 105

Introduction to

SYSTEMS COST-EFFECTIVENESS

INTRODUCTION

The use of cost-effectiveness analyses is today a contractual requirement imposed by the Department of Defense on contractors in the Project Definition Phase of large development projects. As far back as 1965 the President of the United States announced his desire to introduce an integrated Planning-Programming-Budgeting System, similar to that of the Defense Department, in the other agencies of the Executive Branch. The cost-effectiveness analysis is, of course, a basic part of the Planning-Programming-Budgeting System. The adoption of the cost-effectiveness discipline throughout the Executive Branch of the Federal Government is now well established. More recently, several of the state and municipal governments have been actively following the Federal Government's example.

With these impressive accomplishments as a background, it seems appropriate as an introduction to define a cost-effectiveness analysis for the purpose of this book as being that procedure by which the costs of alternative means of achieving a stated effectiveness, or, conversely, the effectiveness of alternative means for a given cost, are compared in a series of numerical indices. The objective of the analysis is to isolate the alternative or combination of alternatives that either gives the greatest expected effectiveness for a given expected cost or a given expected effectiveness for the least expected cost.

It is recognized that a cost-effectiveness analysis does not and cannot mean precisely the same thing to all practitioners in the field. The chief aim of this book is to provide a concise reference to those methods of cost-effectiveness analysis that have been developed and used mostly for large-scale systems. The most appropriate definition of a system for the purpose of this book is given in Webster as, "a group of devices or artificial objects forming a network or used for a common purpose (a nationwide dial telephone system)." This does not mean that the techniques to be described are suitable only for large-scale systems; rather the cost-effectiveness analysis of the simple system or component would merely require a consolidation of the methodology described herein.

It will be apparent to those readers who are students of economics that what is being called a cost-effectiveness analysis is in essence based on nothing more than classic graduate economic theory. The similarity between the two is apparent when one considers a well-accepted definition of economics as being concerned with "the allocation of scarce resources among competing ends to maximize satisfaction."[1]

Although much of the practice in cost-effectiveness analyses has been with military systems, there is no fundamental reason why it is not equally applicable to any other field. As a result the nonmilitary applications are rapidly expanding into many new fields, such as medicine and transportation.[2]

The subject matter has been conveniently divided into four parts. Part I is a wide-angle view of various cost-related factors of particular significance in system cost-effectiveness analyses. Part II describes the structure of system cost models suitable for inclusion in over-all cost-effectiveness models. Part III develops the structure of an effectiveness model based on system performance, availability, reliability, and survivability. Part IV combines the system cost and effectiveness models into over-all cost-effectiveness models ranging from simple ratio models to those with complex probabilistic indifference curves.

Ratio models are limited in that from an array of possible alternatives the model is capable only of isolating a complete system entity as a preferred alternative to all others. In contrast, probabilistic indifference curve models are capable of identifying with statistical significance any combined mixture of system alternatives that may appear better than any other single alternative. Of course, this may not always be the case—that the preferred system configuration is indeed a combination of fractions of alternatives rather than a single whole. The advantage of using the indifference curve cost-effectiveness model (particularly if it is probabilistic) is that if there is a preferred combination of fractions of alternatives it will not pass statistically unnoticed.

It would be amiss to proceed without an admonition concerning the imperfect state of any preferred system configuration, regardless of the type of cost-effectiveness model used for the selection. This simply means that although the model may have indicated a preferred choice, or choices, it must be realized that this preference must always be predi-

[1] For a more detailed statement of the subject matter of economics in this context see Charles J. Hitch and Roland N. McKean, *The Economics of Defense in the Nuclear Age,* Harvard University Press, 1963, pp. 1–3.

[2] See H. E. Klarman, *The Economics of Health,* Columbia University Press, 1965, pp. 162–173, and the Operations Research Society's new quarterly journal, *Transportation Science,* Waverly Press, which began publication in 1967.

cated on less than a complete consideration of all the variables involved. A truly complete analysis would entail isolating all the variables in the system on a global basis, determining their limits, their functions, their relative weights, their interdependence, their time rates of change—in short, an impractical if not completely impossible undertaking that would be in itself the poorest of cost-effectiveness practice, since the cost and time required for such futile attempts in all likelihood would be prohibitive compared with the reduction in the error of the estimates. Most cost-effectiveness models therefore are suboptimizations at best and usually will not be found to contain any second- or higher order terms.

Since the optimum solution is not attainable in the limit, the results must always be a relatively imperfect solution at best. It is in the attainment of an appropriate degree of suboptimization that there will always be found a considerable exercise of judgment. Like it or not, judgment is needed to arrive at what may be considered too much analysis versus what may be considered too little analysis. The very writing of this book involved such considerations. In the final analysis the best that can be hoped for in a world full of uncertainty is a good compromise with the unattainable.

SUGGESTED READINGS

- Hitch, Charles J., and Roland N. McKean. *The Economics of Defense in the Nuclear Age*. Harvard University Press, 1963. A most informative discussion of military problems as being economic problems insofar as they involve the efficient allocation and use of resources.
- McKean, Roland N. *Efficiency in Government through Systems Analysis*. Wiley, New York, 1958. An excellent account of the application of cost-effectiveness principles based on actual government projects.
- Samuelson, Paul A. *Economics,* 7th ed. McGraw-Hill, New York, 1967. A renowned basic text in economics.

General Notation Used in Part I

$$
\begin{aligned}
C &= \text{total system cost} \\
\bar{C} &= \text{average system cost} \\
\bar{C}^* &= \text{cumulative average system cost} \\
\frac{dC}{dQ} &= \text{marginal system cost} \\
F &= \text{total fixed cost} \\
\bar{F} &= \text{average fixed cost} \\
\frac{\partial F}{\partial Q} &= \text{marginal fixed cost} \\
V &= \text{total variable cost} \\
\bar{V} &= \text{average variable cost} \\
\frac{\partial V}{\partial Q} &= \text{marginal variable cost} \\
M &= \text{money} \\
r &= \text{interest rate per year} \\
n &= \text{number of years}
\end{aligned}
$$

Part I

COST FACTORS

The cost-related factors to be described in Part I were chosen with two objectives in mind: (a) to assemble for discussion those cost factors of particular significance in system cost-effectiveness analyses and (b) to provide a tutorial background for Part II in which these cost factors play a key role in cost-model development. The cost factors considered most significant for a system cost-effectiveness analysis are the following:

1. Level of use
2. Inheritance
3. Research and development
4. Input
5. Output
6. Time
7. Performance
8. Geographic location

Each of these factors is discussed in detail with particular emphasis on its significance in a cost-effectiveness analysis.

1. LEVEL OF USE

In considering the cost aspect of a cost-effectiveness analysis, one of the first things to determine is the system's level of use in the organizational hierarchy. This, in turn, will determine the costing level, hence the depth of cost coverage in the program breakdown structure. From a cost standpoint levels of use are cumulative in that at any one in particular there will have to be included in the cost for that level all the costs in all those below. The level of use for costing therefore establishes the number of sublevels encompassed in the cost. An illustrative level of use structure in a military hierarchy may be conveniently pictured by ordering the levels associated with a warning system shown in Table 1.1.

In connection with the level of use it may be well to point out that the higher the level, the greater the tendency for the lower cost levels not to be detailed. Stated another way, the number of levels of cost detail below the level of interest is generally limited so that the bottom layer cost details peel off as the level of interest is raised. In this peeling off process there may well be lost collateral requirements associated

Table 1.1

Level of Use		Illustrative Descriptor
1	Service	United States Air Force
2	Command	North American Air Defense
3	System	Ballistic Missile Early Warning System
4	Subsystem	Radar
5	Module	Receiver
6	Circuit	Amplifier
7	Component	Transistor

with those cost layers not detailed if an inclusiveness check is not made. In the illustration given there is the possibility, for example, of excluding the test equipment necessary to check the performance at the component level.

2. INHERITANCE

Closely associated with the determination of the level of use is the determination of the degree of inheritance that may be available in considering a new system. In the example given, if the level of use has been determined to be the USAF, the consideration of the installation of a new aerospace warning system may conceivably make use of all or part of the USAF's existing or planned bases, communication, data processing, and display facilities. In addition, other activities may be able to provide additional benefits; using the same illustration, a satellite communications system could assist in satisfying the communications requirements imposed by a new warning system. The concept of inheritance leads directly to the concept of incremental cost, which means that only the requirements beyond those that can be inherited are charged to the new system; therefore by definition

$$\text{Total system cost} - \text{inheritance} = \text{incremental system cost.}$$

Inheritance frequently plays an important role in system cost-effectiveness evaluations and in some cases is the only distinguishing characteristic between alternative systems.

The minimization of incremental costs rests on the desire to obtain as much inheritance as possible from existing systems as well as from portions of other systems yet to be implemented. Hitch and McKean discuss the problems of considering the inheritance factor and the use of "opportunity" costs;[1] for example, the use of an inherited asset to achieve any particular future objective may involve "opportunity" costs; meaning, the use of these assets now may make it necessary to forego valuable opportunities of using them later to reach some other future objective. Opportunity cost bears no necessary relation to the historical cost of production: it could be considerably greater or much less. To illustrate, the value of existing land lines for a current need may be much less than their value for some future need; therefore, if a system is to be deployed at present, the future value of the inherited facilities in the alternative use would be charged to the present system. Stated more simply, if you use it now, you cannot use it later and you must pay the price of nonforbearance, whatever that may be.

Although inheritance is normally thought of in terms of tangible assets, the intangible benefits from research and development programs on other systems may also provide significant savings to a new system.

3. RESEARCH AND DEVELOPMENT

The National Science Foundation, one of the most active organizations in R & D data gathering, uses the following definitions of R & D:[2]

BASIC RESEARCH is research in which the primary aim of the investigator is a fuller knowledge or understanding of the subject under study rather than a practical application of it.

APPLIED RESEARCH is directed toward the practical application of knowledge and covers research projects that represent investigations directed toward discovery of new scientific knowledge and have specific commercial objectives with respect to products or processes.

DEVELOPMENT is the systematic use of scientific knowledge directed toward the production of useful materials, devices, systems, or methods, including design and development of prototypes and processes.

The term R & D, as used throughout the remainder of this text, is assumed to embrace all three of these definitions unless otherwise defined.

[1] Charles J. Hitch and Roland N. McKean, *The Economics of Defense in the Nuclear Age,* Harvard University Press, 1963, pp. 26–28.

[2] *Reviews of Data on Research and Development,* National Science Foundation Bulletin 41, Washington, D.C., September, 1963, p. 10.

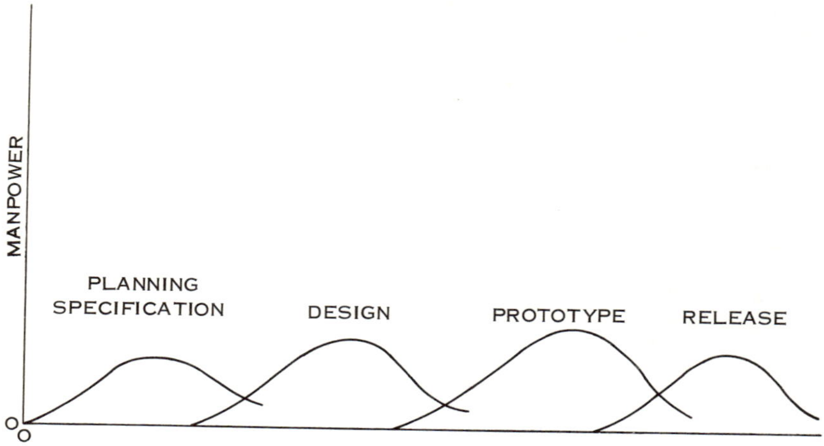

Figure 1.1

A unique expression of the functional relationship between the anatomy of an R & D program and its cost in manpower is given in what has been described as the "Development Life-Cycle Model."[3] A graphical view of the four phases in the life cycle of an R & D program is shown in Figure 1.1.

The equations developed to describe this process are

$$y = k(1 - e^{-at^2}), \tag{1.3.1}$$

$$y' = 2kate^{-at^2}, \tag{1.3.2}$$

where y = cumulative manpower to date,
y' = manpower for each month,
k = total manpower for the cycle,
a = parameter governing the shape of the curve,
t = time from the start of the cycle,
e = 2.71828.

The unique factors that make this model useful are the following:

1. The pattern of each of the four cycles has a high degree of stability.
2. The ratio of size (or manpower requirements) between any one cycle and the next is quite stable and can be predicted.[4] Thus, even

[3] Peter V. Norden, *On the Anatomy of Development Projects,* IRE Transactions on Engineering Management, Vol. EM-7, No. 1. pp. 34–42, New York, March, 1960.
[4] Robert E. Seiler, *Improving the Effectiveness of Research and Development,* McGraw-Hill, New York, 1965, p. 28.

though the k and a factors may not be known at the beginning of a particular project, completion or near completion of the first cycle provides sufficient data for the relatively accurate planning of the remaining three cycles.[5]

There are two general observations worth noting in research and development cost estimating:

1. The greater the desired advance in the state of the art beyond current technology, the greater the estimate of the cost of the R & D required.
2. A corollary to (1) is that the greater the desired advance in the state of the art beyond current technology, the greater the uncertainty of achieving that advance, hence the lower the level in the confidence of the R & D cost estimate.

The combined effect on R & D cost estimating of these two observations is that increasing the advance in the state of the art will result not only in increasing the cost but also in increasing the cost uncertainty.

In Part II on system cost models R & D is discussed again, only not as an estimate derived from a functional relationship but rather as an estimate made by aggregating the individual estimates of each element in an R & D program.

4. INPUTS

Measuring the total cost of a system in terms of the identified factors of production required as inputs is the conventional cost-accounting approach based on the market values of those input units. These factors represent the material, labor, and capital combined in a transformation of the material factor into the output representing the total cost of the system. Included in the total system cost, of course, is a pro rata provision for the recovery of the costs of administration, distribution, and a return on capital. Functionally, the process may be represented by the production function for a single firm, which may be written as[6]

$$C = f(m, l, c), \tag{1.4.1}$$

where C = total system cost,
m = material,
l = labor,
c = capital.

[5] *Ibid.*

[6] See Lawrence R. Klein, *An Introduction to Econometrics*, Prentice-Hall, Englewood Cliffs, N.J., 1962, pp. 83–125.

No further discussion of the synthesis of total system cost as a function of input factor units is made here in Part I, since it is developed in much greater detail in Part II.

5. OUTPUT

Total, Variable, Fixed, Average, Marginal Costs

Costs may be categorized in terms of their sensitivity to changes in output. Changes in output, of course, entail changes in time, but changes in time do not necessarily result in changes in output. Costs that change with output (e.g., product packing) will also be changing with time, but costs that change with time (e.g., rent) do not necessarily result in a change in output.

In the long run the economist views all costs as variable. Cost-effectiveness analyses, however, are predominantly short run in nature, hence must assume within their scope a constituent of fixed cost.

Beginning with the concept of a total system cost C, the components thereof classified in terms of sensitivity to output Q are

$$\begin{aligned}
&\text{total system cost} &&= C, \quad dC/dQ > 0, < \infty \\
&\text{total fixed cost} &&= F, \quad dF/dQ = 0 \\
&\text{total variable cost} &&= V, \quad dV/dQ > 0, < \infty \\
&\text{average system cost} &&= \bar{C}, \quad d\bar{C}/dQ > 0, < \infty \\
&\text{average fixed cost} &&= \bar{F}, \quad d\bar{F}/dQ > 0, < \infty \\
&\text{average variable cost} &&= \bar{V}, \quad d\bar{V}/dQ > 0, < \infty
\end{aligned}$$

These cost components are related as follows:

$$C = F + V = \sum_{i=1}^{m} F_i + \sum_{i=1}^{n} V_i, \tag{1.5.1}$$

where i = cost of ith component.

$$\bar{C} = \frac{C}{Q} = \bar{F} + \bar{V} = \frac{F}{Q} + \frac{V}{Q} = \left[\sum_{i=1}^{m} F_i\right]\Big/Q + \left[\sum_{i=1}^{n} V_i\right]\Big/Q, \tag{1.5.2}$$

$$\frac{dC}{dQ} = \frac{\partial F}{\partial Q} + \frac{\partial V}{\partial Q}. \tag{1.5.3}$$

The distinction between the total system cost C, the average system cost $\bar{C}$, and the marginal system cost dC/dQ may be seen in the cost schedule in Table 1.2.

Table 1.2

Unit	Total = $C = \sum_{i=1}^{n} C_i$	Average = $\bar{C} = \frac{C}{n}$	Marginal = $\frac{dC}{dQ}$
1	40	40	40
2	90	45	50
3	135	45	45
4	160	40	25

The following observations may be made concerning the entries in this schedule:

1. *The First Units.* The cumulative, the average, and the marginal costs for the first unit are equal.

2. *The Relation Between the Cumulative and the Marginal Costs.* The cumulative cost is always the sum of the preceding marginal costs.

3. *The Interaction Between the Average and the Marginal Costs.* For the average to rise the marginal costs must be $>$ the average; for the average to remain unchanged the average and the marginal costs must be equal; for the average to fall the marginal cost must be $<$ the average.

The various components of total system cost C are shown graphically in Figure 1.2.

The geometry of Figure 1.2 shows the following:

1. Given any point A on a cumulative curve, the corresponding average $\bar{C}$ at that point is the slope of the straight line, OA, which connects point A with the origin.

$$\bar{C} = \text{slope} = \frac{\text{ordinate}}{\text{abscissa}} = \frac{AQ1}{OQ1}.$$

The same relationship is applicable to points B and C and by deduction to any point along any cumulative curve.

2. Given any point A on a cumulative curve, the marginal dC/dQ is equal to the slope of the curve at point A. The same relationship

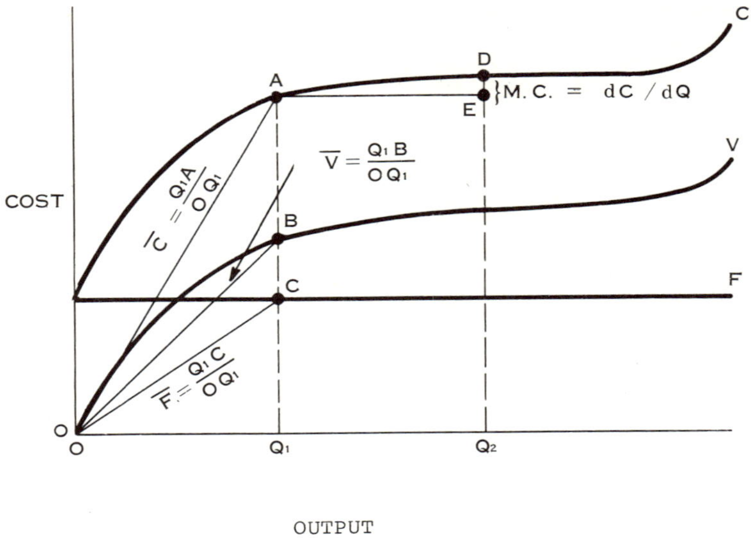

Figure 1.2

is applicable to points B and C and by deduction to any point along any cumulative curve.

$$\frac{dC}{dQ} = \text{slope} = \frac{\text{ordinate}}{\text{abscissa}} = \frac{DE}{AE}.$$

The relationship between the marginal and the average curves is shown in Figure 1.3.

The geometry of Figure 1.3 shows the following:

1. Since the total cost equals the average cost per unit times the number of units, then the total cost of output $OQ_1 = OQ_1 \times Q_1R$, which is the area of the rectangle OQ_1RS.

2. The total cost of output OQ_1 is also equal to OQ_1TC, that is, $CSW = WTR$.

The relationship between the straight-line marginal and the average curves is shown in Figure 1.4.

Given any straight-line average curve, the corresponding marginal curve is a straight line that originates where the average curve crosses the ordinate axis and cuts through the midpoint of any horizontal line to the average curve, as shown in Figure 1.4.

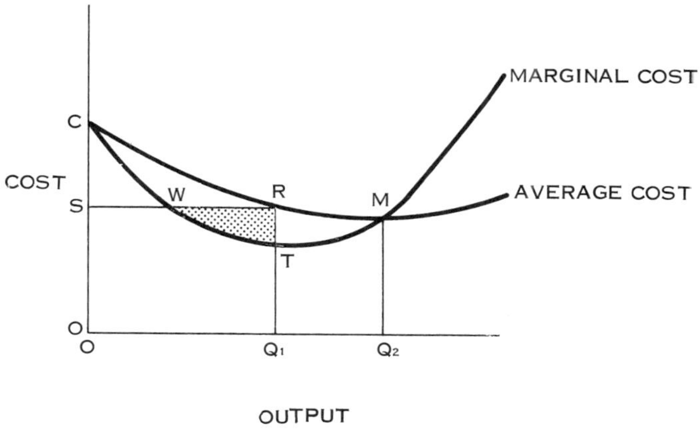

Figure 1.3

To find the marginal curve to an average curve *that is not straight,* draw a straight line tangent to the average curve at some output Q; find the corresponding marginal line to this tangent as described above and thereby find the marginal point on that line at output Q. Form a sufficient number of such points over the range of the output so that their locus, which is the marginal curve, is reasonably well defined.

Optimal Return Output versus Optimal Efficiency Output

The output of an activity should, if possible, be expanded only as long as the marginal benefit exceeds the marginal cost. The expansion should be stopped at that point at which the marginal net yield is zero. This is the optimal net return output as shown at point 6 in Figure 1.5; further expansion simply invites a marginal net loss (points 7 and

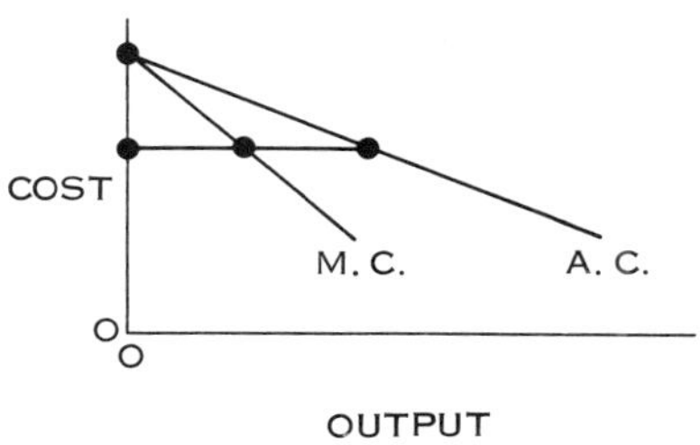

Figure 1.4

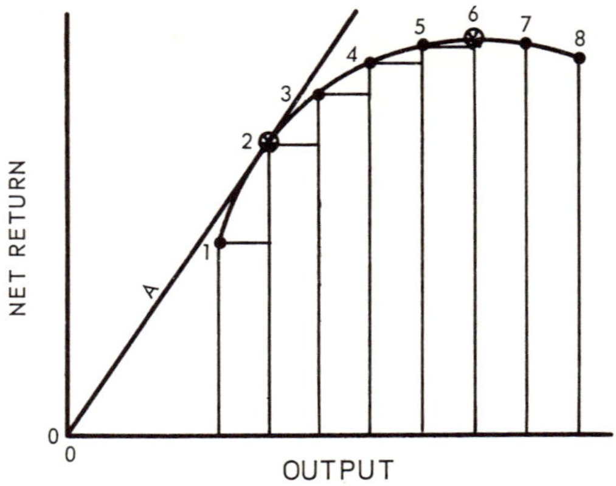

Figure 1.5

8). The basis for this claim is found in the calculus proposition: to maximize any $y = f(x)$ it is necessary that the first derivative dy/dx (the marginal or differential effect of x on y) be zero.

If, however, the objective function being maximized is efficiency (defined as the highest ratio of net return to output), point 2 would be optimal, since its coordinates coincide with that vector **A** from the origin whose slope is maximum, as shown in Figure 1.5.

Relative Activity Levels

For optimal results different activities should, whenever possible be carried to levels at which all yield the same marginal returns per unit of effort (cost). Reallocating some of the resources from an activity with a smaller marginal return to one with a larger marginal return will therefore improve the over-all yield.

Breakeven Point

Another way of analyzing cost as a function of output is to observe the intersection of the cumulative effectiveness or revenue curve and the cumulative cost curve, known as the breakeven point. A breakeven analysis is of particular significance to a cost-effectiveness analysis when the ratios of the fixed cost to the variable cost are widely different among the competing alternatives; for example, consider two systems that have the same revenue or effectiveness curve E and also reach the same total system cost C, the only difference being the ratio of fixed (investment) cost F to variable (operating) cost V, as shown in

Figure 1.6*a* and *b*. The observations of interest in Figure 1.6 are given in Table 1.3.

Even though two systems may have the same revenue or effectiveness curve and the same ultimate total system cost, their net profit or benefit

Table 1.3

	Figure 1.6*a*	Figure 1.6*b*
Dominant cost	Fixed cost	Variable cost
Breakeven point	Later, higher	Earlier, lower
Net effectiveness area	Smaller	Larger
$\theta = f(dE/dC)$	Larger	Smaller

over time, the rate of change in their net profit or benefit, and their breakeven points may be widely different. Systems dominated by fixed cost therefore would be relatively less desirable than systems dominated by variable cost in situations in which a rapid growth to net effectiveness is essential.

The breakeven point analysis is also of use in resolving decisions between the rental or purchase of equipment. The curves in Figure 1.6 would appear the same; the presentation in *a* representing the purchase alternative and *b* representing the rental alternative.

Short-Run, Long-Run Cost

The results of a cost-effectiveness analysis may be significantly affected by variations in the number of systems to be produced. A simple means of measuring these effects from a cost standpoint is to examine the individual firm's average cost performance as a function of output.

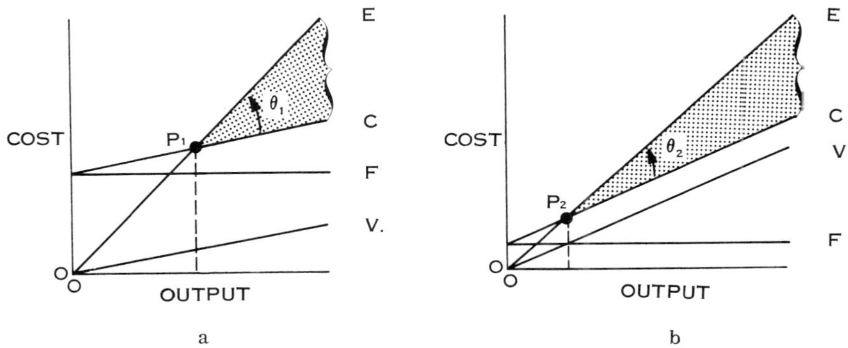

Figure 1.6

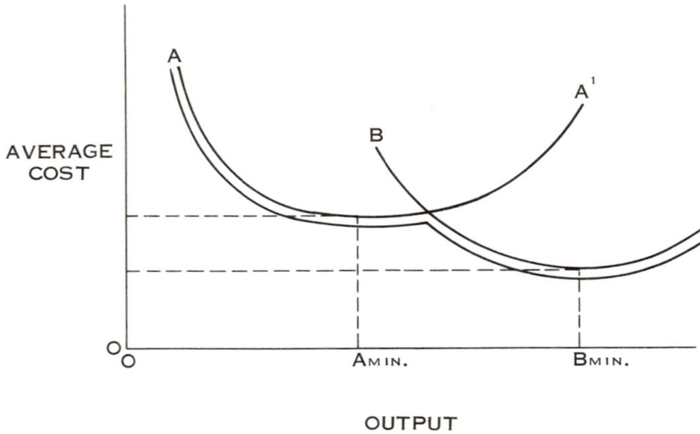

Figure 1.7

Figure 1.7 graphically depicts the normal short-run long-run situation of a firm considering two plants with different average cost curves.

If the firm's demand for systems is estimated to be in the vicinity of $A_{min'}$, plant B can be eliminated from consideration. If, however, the firm's demand for systems is estimated to reach the vicinity of $B_{min'}$ plant A can be eliminated from consideration. The two U-shaped curves are the short-run alternatives available to the firm. The lowest segment of both curves represents the long-run average cost curve for the firm. The distinction between the short-run and the long-run cases in effect pivots on the point in time when the decision is made between the two alternatives in Table 1.4. The number of systems to be produced therefore can have an important bearing on whether the costs to be incurred will be based on the short-run or the long-run cost curves of the firm.

Table 1.4

Point in Time	Nature of Decision
Before choice of plant is made	Long-run
After choice of plant is made	Short-run

6. TIME

Although there are numerous cost functions of time that might be significant in a cost-effectiveness analysis (such as depreciation, obsolescence, and residual value), there are two that are singled out here for discussion. The reason for not discussing the others mentioned is that they are relatively well-established and recognized concepts familiar to most cost analysts and therefore it is not necessary to expand them. The two functions to be discussed, however, are somewhat removed from the recognized and accepted status of the others: (a) discounted cost and (b) obtainability cost.

Discounted Cost

There are two generally acknowledged reasons for discounting future costs. The first is to give recognition to the fact that in general a present monetary unit is worth less than a future monetary unit; and, since it is worth less, it follows that procurement of that unit in the present will cost less than procurement of it in the future. There are several well founded arguments advanced to support this position.[7] Probably the most fundamental argument proposed is based on the payment of interest on borrowed money. For example, consider an individual borrowing money at a bank on a discounted note and having to pay it back at a future time plus the discount. The borrower in this case is willing to accept less money immediately in exchange for more money to be repaid in the future. Such a process may be described by the following equation:

$$M_t = M_{t+n}(1 + r)^{-n}, \tag{1.6.1}$$

where M_t = money borrowed at present time (t),
M_{t+n} = money to be repaid at a future time ($t + n$)
r = interest rate per year,
n = number of years.

For a system funded annually over a period of years a serial process of discounting would be more apropos, as described by the equation

$$C_t = \sum_{i=1}^{n} C_i(1 + r)^{-n}, \tag{1.6.2}$$

where C_t = total system cost at present time (t),
C_i = sum of costs during ith period.

Equation 1.6.2 simply describes the process by which the various discount factors $(1 + r)^{-n}$ are multiplied by the sum of the cost of each period and the resulting products added. Equation 1.6.2 in the limiting

[7] See Hitch, pp. 205–218.

case, in which the discounting would be done continuously rather than discretely, is rewritten as

$$C_t = \sum_{i=1}^{\infty} C_i(e)^{-rn}, \tag{1.6.3}$$

where $e = 2.71828$ (base of Napierian logarithm).

The other basic reason acknowledged for the discounting of future costs rests on the recognition that a system frequently provides collateral benefits to other systems and therefore should be credited for this service. It is interesting to note that if the alternatives have the same ratio of fixed cost to variable cost, regardless of the reason for discounting, the discounting will not affect their relative costs, ceteris paribus.

The discounting of costs has always been a somewhat controversial matter, and even more controversial within the controversy is agreement on what is an appropriate rate to use for discounting. There is really no reason, for the purpose of this book, to go into the merits of the various arguments for different rates of discounting or into the various claims for or against discounting, since those interested will find an excellent discussion of these matters in Hitch![8]

Obtainability Cost

Although the previous concept of discounting future costs resulted in a cost decrease, the concept of the cost of obtainability results in a cost increase. That the combination of the two might be traded off and result in a standoff is a distinct possibility, thereby lending credence to a do-nothing attitude in such cases.

In the cost-effectiveness analysis that involves alternatives with different dates of obtainability some rational method should be employed to quantize this variable. One method suggested by the author consists of penalizing those alternatives that have later obtainability dates by raising their costs by the same compounding technique used previously to discount the cost. Therefore (1.6.1), (1.6.2), and (1.6.3) would be rewrittten with positive exponents:

$$M_t = M_{t+n}(1 + r)^n, \tag{1.6.4}$$

$$C_t = \sum_{i=1}^{n} C_i(1 + r)^n, \tag{1.6.5}$$

$$C_t = \sum_{i=1}^{\infty} C_i(e)^{rn}. \tag{1.6.6}$$

[8] *Ibid.*

This approach is based on the concept of a negative interest. The borrower is now paid to borrow rather than paying to borrow. The rationale for the case of a negative interest in a system cost-effectiveness analysis is based on the dispropensity to wait for the additional performance and/or the lower cost obtainable from those systems with the later obtainability dates. By waiting additional losses and/or costs might be incurred, the effects of which should be recognized. In effect, $-$ is a measure of the rate of dispropensity to wait per period (for whatever lower cost and/or additional performance might be available in the future).

7. PERFORMANCE

The measurement of the cost of a system in terms of the system's performance parameters is usually based on a statistical regression technique. The general procedure is first to determine which parameters have a significant effect on the system cost. This is done by means of sensitivity analyses, using statistical correlation measures. Next, combinations of parameters are tested to determine whether improvements in the coefficient of correlation can be effected over that obtainable with any single parameter. Then, that combination of parameters with the highest coefficient of correlation (or, if no combination excels, that single parameter with the highest coefficient of correlation) is used to construct a regression equation. The net result is an expression of the functional relationship between a system's parameters and its cost. A popular expression for this method is known as the CER (cost estimating relationship).

An example from a RAND Corporation study, which used a multivariable cost-estimating relationship for an airborne radio communication system based on the product of the power output and carrier frequency, is shown in the following equation[9]:

$$\bar{C}^* = KP^x, \tag{1.7.1}$$

where $\bar{C}^* =$ cumulative average cost per unit $= \sum_{i=1}^{n} \bar{C}_i$,

$K =$ constant,

$P =$ product of power output and carrier frequency,

$x =$ exponent.

[9] J. P. Large, *Concepts and Procedures of Cost Analysis,* RM-3589-PR, The RAND Corporation, June 1963, p. XIII–16.

In the example cited the product of the power output and the carrier frequency resulted in a better coefficient of correlation than that obtainable by using either variable separately. The measurement of performance itself, as one of the determinants of system effectiveness, is discussed in greater detail in Part III.

8. GEOGRAPHIC LOCATION

Whenever systems are to be deployed on a global basis, the cost increase in a distant land can become appreciable. An indication of the magnitude of the change in cost as a function of a change in geographic location may be seen by comparing the construction cost multipliers for the continental United States with those for the state of Alaska (see Table 1.5).

Table 1.5

Geographic Area	Construction Cost Multiplier[a]
Continental United States	0.90 → 1.15 depending on exact location
Alaska	1.70 → 3.00 depending on exact location

[a] *Military Construction Pricing Guide,* AFP 88–16, Dept. of the Air Force, March 1967.

The *Military Construction Pricing Guide* contains construction-cost data on most of the countries of the world as well as for each of the states of the United States. Other system costs for packing, transportation, emplacement, installation, test, and operation would also increase above stateside levels for overseas deployment. A significant portion of the so-called standard domestic cost of a system which is to be deployed in a distant land would therefore be affected by a geographic relocation.

The integration of much of the subject matter just reviewed takes place next in Part II which describes the structure of system cost models.

SUGGESTED READINGS

• Baumol, William J. *Economic Theory and Operations Analysis,* 2nd ed. Prentice-Hall, Englewood Cliffs, N.J., 1965. A comprehensive treatment of the application of economic theory to the solution of business problems via operations research.

- Dean, Joel. *Managerial Economics.* Prentice-Hall, Englewood Cliffs, N.J., 1951. A well-regarded text in applied economics recommended particularly for its treatment of cost.
- Klein, Lawrence R. *An Introduction to Econometrics.* Prentice-Hall, Englewood Cliffs, N.J., 1962. An excellent source for a review of the field of econometrics or as an introduction to advanced work.
- Klein, Lawrence R. *An Introduction to Econometrics.* Prentice-Hall, Englewood Cliffs, N.J., 1953. An original work in econometrics recommended particularly for advanced study.

General Notation Used in Part II

R = research and development
I = investment
O = operation
H = inheritance
S = scrap
$\alpha, \beta, \gamma, \xi$ = coefficients of value added
$E(c)$ = expected value of cost component
$V(c)$ = variance of cost component
$E(C)$ = expected value of total system cost
$V(C)$ = variance of total system cost

Part II

SYSTEM COST MODELS

It is the purpose in Part II to develop the structure of system cost models. These models are especially adapted to the measurement of the expected value of total system cost in cost-effectiveness analyses. The system cost model should ideally represent the cost analog of all the elements of a system, from inception to retirement. Pragmatically, however, the system cost model should not be made too detailed lest it become unmanageable, yet it should not be made too general lest it become insensitive to significant system parameters. It is felt that the models to be described represent a good compromise between these extremes. As discussed in Part I, the determination of the structure of a system element depends on the level of use, which in turn defines the costing level and thereunder the system's elements. The output of a system cost model is the result of an integration of the costs of all the elements in the system. This integrated output may be a single expected value or a frequency distribution of values representing the probability density function of the cost of system ownership.

1. MATRIX MODEL

The foundation of all system cost-model development is the arrangement of the appropriate elements of cost into a matrix format. The organization of such a matrix provides a most convenient means of systematically analyzing and synthesizing the cost elements. The cost matrix is usually formed by arraying the cost elements into a two-dimensional field consisting of physical functions juxtaposed with cost functions, as shown in Figure 2.1.

There is an inherent advantage in first preparing a cost matrix for use in a system cost-effectiveness analysis:

2-3

SYSTEM COST MATRIX MODEL

PHASE	PHYSICAL FUNCTIONS	COST FUNCTIONS			
	Modules	Equipment e	Maintenance m	Administration a	Totals
R & D	#1 Module . . . m				Σ . . . Σ
	Total R&D	Σ	Σ	Σ	$\Sigma\Sigma = R$
INVESTMENT	#1 Module . . . m				Σ . . . Σ
	Total Investment	Σ	Σ	Σ	$\Sigma\Sigma = I$
ANNUAL OPERATION	#1 Module . . . m				Σ . . . Σ
	Total Operation	Σ	Σ	Σ	$\Sigma\Sigma$
Operation	Total Oper. x (N $_n$ Yrs.	$N\Sigma$	$n\Sigma$	$n\Sigma$	$n\Sigma\Sigma = O$
R&D + Inv.	Total R&D + Inv.				R + I
All	Total System Cost				R + I + O

Figure 2.1

It provides a checklist of the cost functions and physical functions to be considered, thereby pinpointing possible areas of overlap or omission.

Although the system cost matrix illustrated could become rather extensive in the number of elements it contained, the actual method of working with such a matrix may consist initially of grouping various elements together to reduce the total number to be estimated. Not only is it often less effort to use this shortcut, but in some cases it may be a more representative approach; for example, a composite of the costs for maintenance m and administration a in Figure 2.1 might be derived as a function of the equipment costs e:

$$m + a = f(e) \tag{2.1.1}$$

The point is that each element in the system's cost matrix need not represent a separate effort in cost synthesis. Normally, as a study progresses, the costs of additional elements evolve from the various engineering groups in the firm. A comparison of these later costs with those initially obtained by an aggregation procedure such as (2.1.1) provides a good means of corroborating the original estimates.

2. COST OF ELEMENTS

The next phase in system cost-model development is the derivation of the means for estimating the cost of each element in the cost matrix. Two basic approaches may be used to derive the costs of the elements in a total system cost aggregation:

1. *Statistical Correlation*

(a) The cost of an element may be determined by a regression of its design parameters with the historical costs of the same or similar type

(2.2.1)

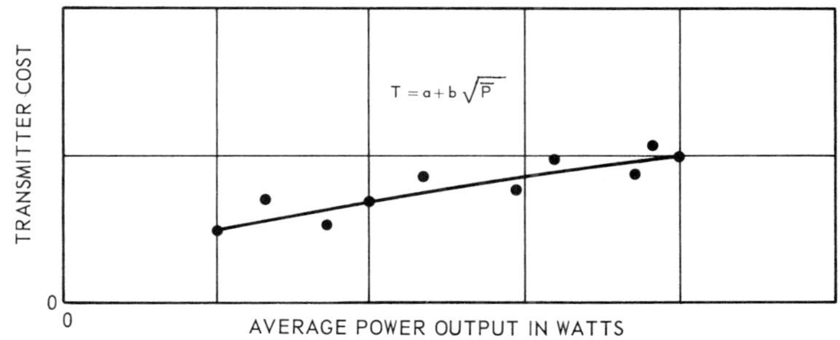

Figure 2.2

(2.2.2.)

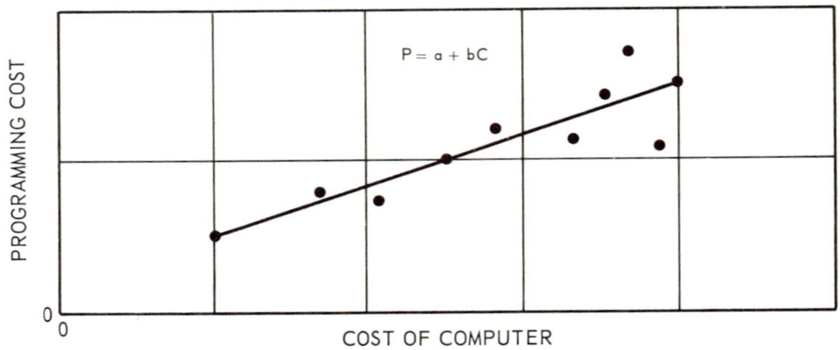

Figure 2.3

elements, thereby forming a cost analog over some range of the elements' design parameters[1]; for example, the cost of a transmitter T may be described in terms of a range of designed average power output $\bar{P}$ in watts as shown in Figure 2.2.

(b) The cost of an element may be determined by a regression of its cost with the cost of an associated element, thereby forming a cost analog of some other element's cost; for example, the cost of a computer program P may be described in terms of the cost of computers C, as shown in Figure 2.3.

The terms a and b in (2.2.1) and (2.2.2) are the regression equation constants. The deviations about the curve in Figure 2.2 show a uniform dispersion (homoscedastic), whereas the deviations about the curve in Figure 2.3 exhibit a tendency to increasing dispersion as the cost of the computer increases (heteroscedastic). The actual regression technique, based on least squares theory, consists of finding that trend line through the points which results in the sum of the squared deviations from the trend line being a minimum. These deviations may be measured in one of three basic directions of displacement[2]:

(a) Vertically, which is a minimization of the sum of the squared vertical deviations.

[1] The distinction between performance and design parameters is brought to attention at this point because later in Part III on system effectiveness the basic design is derated to reflect the actual realized design in the operating environment.

[2] For a detailed discussion of these methods of regression analysis see Lawrence R. Klein, *A Textbook of Econometrics,* Prentice-Hall, Englewood Cliffs, N.J., 1953, pp. 282–322.

(b) Horizontally, which is a minimization of the sum of the squared horizontal deviations.

(c) Perpendicularly, which is a minimization of the sum of the squared orthogonal deviations.

Both statistical correlation techniques are better known as CER's (cost estimating relationships), which were described briefly in Part I; CER's have three fundamental uses in the synthesis of a total system cost:

(a) As a means of generating the cost of a system's elements in the absence of other means.

(b) As a means of documenting other means of preparing the cost of a system's elements.

(c) As a means of generating changes in the cost of a system's elements as a function of performance-parameter changes in the conduct of tradeoff and sensitivity analyses.

2. *Mathematical Summation*

The cost of an element may be determined by mathematically summing the various components of its cost. To illustrate the procedure three examples of equations, which could be used to derive the cost of, say, the No. 1 module element in Figure 2.1 for the R & D, investment, and annual operation phases, are given as the following:

(a) R & D Phase

$$R_{\text{el}} = (E_s + E_h + E_r + E_m + E_c + E_e), \tag{2.2.3}$$

where R_{el} = research and development (No. 1 module equipment),
E_s = engineering, systems,
E_h = engineering, human factors,
E_r = engineering, reliability,
E_m = engineering, mechanical,
E_c = engineering, civil,
E_e = engineering, economics.

(b) Investment Phase

$$I_{\text{el}} = E_d + E_p + D + T + (M + L) \exp Q + S + F + X + Y + Z, \tag{2.2.4}$$

where I_{el} = investment (No. 1 module equipment),
E_d = engineering, design,
E_p = engineering, project,
D = drafting,
T = tooling,

M = material, factory,
L = labor, factory,
Q = learning curve factor,
S = spares,
F = freight,
X = emplacement,
Y = installation,
Z = test.

(c) Operation Phase

$$O_{\text{el}} = (S + W + L + P + C_c), \tag{2.2.5}$$

where O_{el} = operation (No. 1 module equipment),
S = spares,
W = spares depot including logistic support,
L = labor,
P = power or fuel,
C_c = communication channels.

In Equations 2.2.3 to 2.2.5 the standard prorata costs for overhead, general and administrative expense, advertising, royalties, and profit have been omitted for simplicity.

The maintenance (m) and administrative (a) cost functions for the system may be similarly derived or functionally related to the equipment cost (e) through a statistical correlation, either as a group [see (2.1.1)] or as separate functions of each item of equipment.

3. MODEL EXPANSION

The matrix format, described above, of a system cost model is quite manageable whenever the actual work is to be done by hand. For very large systems, however, hand solutions become impractical and it becomes necessary to go to a machine computation. It then becomes desirable to describe the cost model in terms of a mathematical notation that will facilitate the computer programming process.

It is helpful beforehand to show the over-all view of the mathematical structure of a large-scale system cost model by arranging the major cost categories in a time flow chart, as shown in Figure 2.4. In essence, the arrangement represents a sequential input-output flow chart. It will be noted that inheritance and scrap value are specifically programmed here for machine computation, whereas with hand-solution models the investment category is better carried as a net item to reduce the computations.

TIME FLOW CHART OF MAJOR COST CATEGORIES
IN LARGE SCALE SYSTEMS COST MODELS

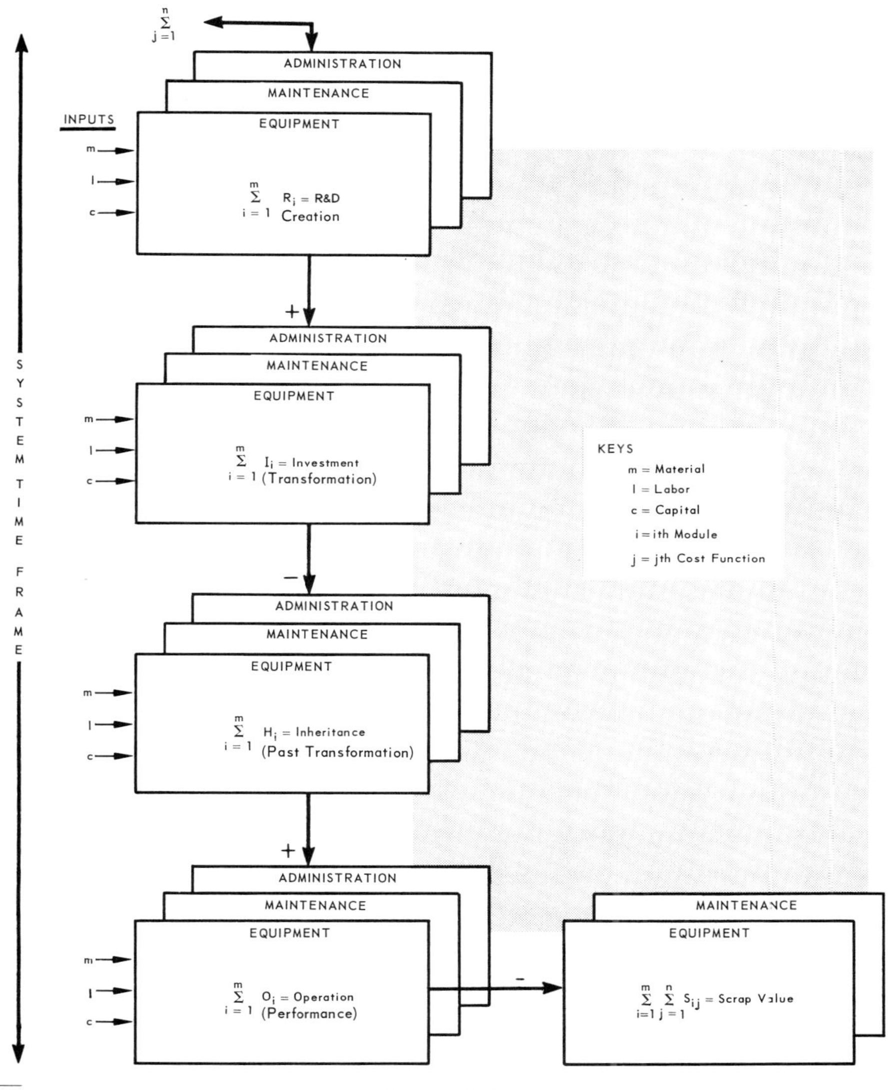

Figure 2.4

Based on the relationships shown in Figure 2.4, the total system cost C may be expressed as follows:

$$
\begin{aligned}
(2.3.1)\quad C = {} & \alpha\Big[\Big(\sum_{i=1}^{m}\sum_{j=1}^{n} R_m\Big) + \Big(\sum_{i=1}^{m}\sum_{j=1}^{n} R_l\Big) + \Big(\sum_{i=1}^{m}\sum_{j=1}^{n} R_c\Big)\Big] \\
& + \beta\Big[\Big(\sum_{i=1}^{m}\sum_{j=1}^{n} I_m\Big) + \Big(\sum_{i=1}^{m}\sum_{j=1}^{n} I_l\Big) + \Big(\sum_{i=1}^{m}\sum_{j=1}^{n} I_c\Big)\Big] \\
& - \gamma\Big[\Big(\sum_{i=1}^{m}\sum_{j=1}^{n} H_m\Big) + \Big(\sum_{i=1}^{m}\sum_{j=1}^{n} H_l\Big) + \Big(\sum_{i=1}^{m}\sum_{j=1}^{n} H_c\Big)\Big] \\
& + \xi\Big[\Big(\sum_{i=1}^{m}\sum_{j=1}^{n} O_m\Big) + \Big(\sum_{i=1}^{m}\sum_{j=1}^{n} O_l\Big) + \Big(\sum_{i=1}^{m}\sum_{j=1}^{n} O_c\Big)\Big] \\
& - \Big[\sum_{i=1}^{m}\sum_{j=1}^{n} S_{ij}\Big],
\end{aligned}
$$

where α, β, γ, ξ = coefficients of value added (used to raise input values to user cost level),

R = research and development = total cost incurred before production,

I = investment = total cost incurred in production,

O = operation = total cost incurred in use subsequent to production until scrapped,

H = inheritance = total cost saved by utilizing resources made available by and charged to other programs,

S = scrap value = residual value at end of useful life,

m = material,
l = labor,
c = capital,
i = ith module,
j = jth cost function.

Equation 2.3.1 may be readily converted into any number of standard computer program languages which will set up the necessary machine registers, indexers, accumulators, adders, subtractors, subroutines, and so forth. As a matter of practice it has become customary to express system cost models in mathematical notation, regardless of whether the analysis is going to be run on a computer. The mathematical notation is in itself an excellent means by which to grasp the comprehensiveness of a system in a language that is understood by practitioners from many disciplines.

4. MINIMIZING TOTAL SYSTEM COST

Regardless of whether a system cost model is to be "run" by hand or machine, the first phase in any optimization procedure should be an examination of the various alternatives for possible tradeoffs between the R & D, the investment, and the annual operation. This preliminary optimization procedure may often save much subsequent computation of nonoptimized inputs.

Total system cost may frequently be reduced without changing the effectiveness by merely adjusting the balance between the R & D and investment and operation; for example, additional R & D expenditures may be more than offset in reduced operational costs by greater automation but at the sacrifice of a longer lead time due to the additional R & D. For those systems that are effectively free of any constraints an optimization of the constituents of total system cost may be made so that their sum is a minimum:

$$C = R + I + O = \text{min.} \tag{2.4.1}$$

Equation 2.4.1 requires that the first order partial derivatives of each of the variables with respect to the function being minimized be zero:

$$\frac{\partial C}{\partial R} = 0, \tag{2.4.2}$$

$$\frac{\partial C}{\partial I} = 0, \tag{2.4.3}$$

$$\frac{\partial C}{\partial O} = 0 \tag{2.4.4}$$

Whenever (2.4.1) is subject to any real constraint, a limited minimization may still be carried out, subject to that constraint. A more detailed discussion of this type of operation is reserved for Part III, in which both minimization and maximization procedures are outlined.

5. PERIOD COSTING

Period costing is the most commonly used method of comparing the costs of alternative systems over time. It simply represents the summary

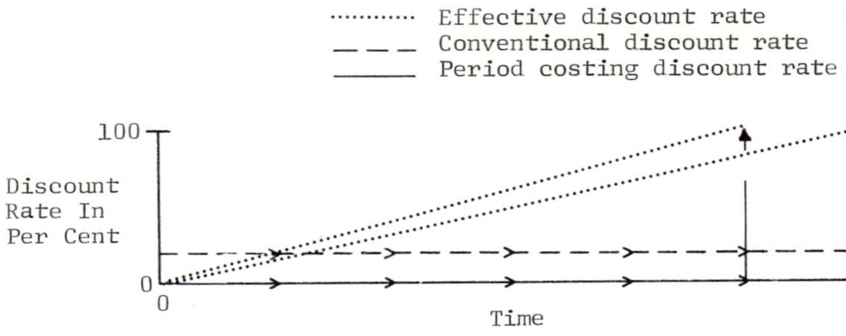

Figure 2.5

of all the system's costs for a fixed period of time, including R & D, investment, and the annual operating costs. Frequently used periods are 5, 10 and 20 years. The natural life expectancy of the system, of course, has a strong influence on the length of the period used.

The use of period costing is somewhat analogous to discounting at a rate which, in effect, continuously increases from zero to 100 percent, as shown by the dotted lines in Figure 2.5. Instead of conventionally discounting at some constant rate per unit of time (usually a year) in period costing, the discount rate is zero throughout the period and rises instantly to 100 percent at the very end, as shown by the lowest line in Figure 2.5.

The effect of lengthening the period, therefore, in a period-costing analysis is to decrease the effective discount rate at any discrete point in time within the period (vertical distance between the dotted lines).

Similarly, the effect of the salvage value in a period-costing analysis will also cause the effective discount rate to decrease, as shown in Figure 2.6.

Another use made of period costing is to test the sensitivity of a preferred system to changes in the total costing time period. The effect of accelerating a system's development as well as stretching out a system's program can thereby be determined beforehand.

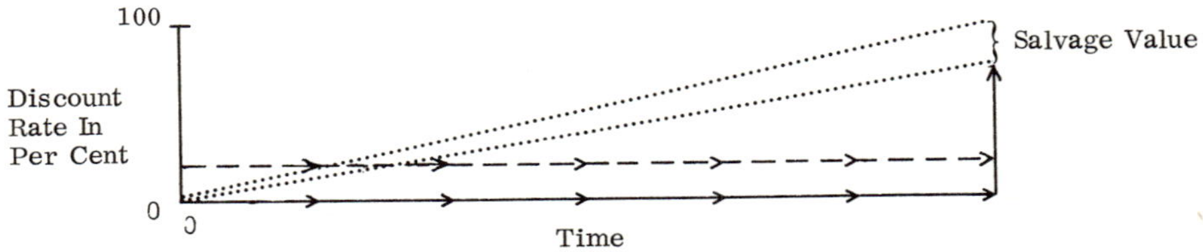

Figure 2.6

6. TIME PHASING

Regardless of the costing period chosen, it is often desirable to time phase the total system cost throughout the total time period. The time phasing of system costs refers to a procedure by which the frequency or density of cost per unit of time (one year or less) is recorded on a continuous time scale. In this format the sequence of system events, beginning with the research and development and ending with the annual operations, is shown in clear relative time phase positions. Frequent uses of the time-phased total-system cost diagram are (a) to permit the visualization of the tradeoffs possible between the R & D, the investment and the annual operation; (b) to permit inter- as well as intrasystem cost/time comparisons; (c) to identify critical funding periods; (d) to identify areas of functional overlap requiring matched interfaces for effective transition. A typical time-phased total-system cost diagram is shown in Figure 2.7.

It may be seen in Figure 2.7 that the "busiest" phase occurs in the fabrication of the system because it overlaps a portion of every other phase in the program. By changing the ordinate scale of Figure 2.7 to read both positive and negative the relative time phases may be assigned a polarity, thereby producing the so-called cash-flow diagram in which the R & D through test phases would become cash-out (—) and the annual operations, net cash-in (+).

7. FIXED COST PRORATION

Time phasing, of course, will not affect the amount of fixed cost to be charged to each unit produced. Fixed costs, however, are a problem in

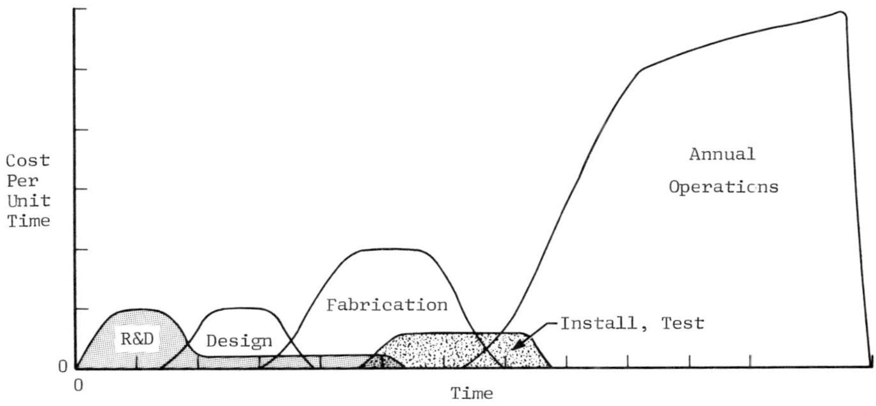

Figure 2.7

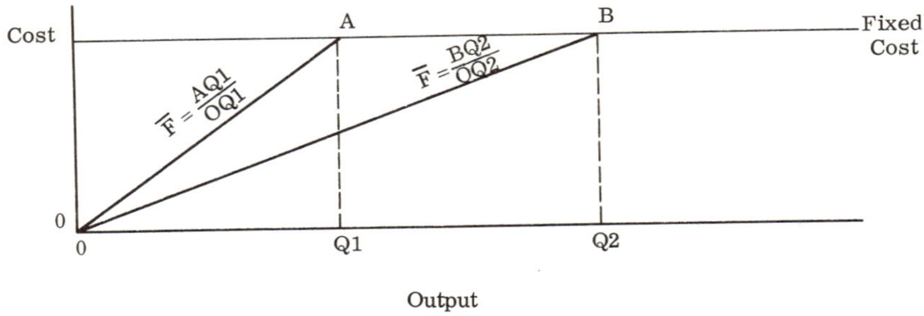

Figure 2.8

cost analyses whenever the effects of quantity changes are being measured. This is because the fixed cost must be prorated (divided) by the various quantities being considered in order to obtain the average fixed cost $\bar{F}$ to charge to each unit (see Figure 2.8).

A system dominated by high fixed costs will be relatively more sensitive to quantity changes than a system with a relatively low fixed cost, as described in Part I under the breakeven point. When the alternatives being compared contain many subsystems, each with varying ratios of fixed to variable costs, the computation problem can become very involved and may be more readily handled on a computer either as a specific program or as part of an over-all system cost model program.

The amount of fixed cost to be allocated to a new system should reflect a realistic allocation of only those fixed costs that remain unabsorbed before the new system commitment. This is a frequently overlooked error which may result in considerable inflation of the measure of investment in a new system.

8. VARIABLE COST NONLINEARITY

In the discussion so far it has been tacitly assumed that all variable costs would vary linearly with the quantity of systems produced. Variable costs that are linear with production quantity present no particular problem in computation; however, nonlinear variable costs need to be defined with respect to their functional (mathematical) relationship to the quantity of systems produced. There are two basic approaches to the handling of nonlinear variable costs:

1. Divide the nonlinear cost curve into several segments small enough to be considered linear, as shown in Figure 2.9. Observe that the expo-

nentially downward sloping heavy line may be reasonably approximated by a combination of segments from the three straight lines, a–b, c–d, e–f.

Obviously, the larger the number of segments that can be used in a given approximation, the better the fit that can be made. Naturally, a tradeoff is involved here between the effort required in additional segmentation and the reduction in the error of the fit.

2. The other basic approach to the handling of nonlinear variable cost/quantity relationships is to attempt to derive a mathematical equation that appears to fit the data most accurately. The reader is cautioned in such an endeavor to be aware that the derivation of a mathematical expression to fit certain nonlinear functions may become an exercise that requires considerable skill in numerical mathematical analysis techniques. No attempt is made here to cover the vast amount of material that would be necessary to develop such mathematical procedures.[3] It may be stated, however, that in general nonlinear expressions of the cubic form may provide reasonably good fits in many cases. A cubic equation that could be used to approximate the curve in Figure 2.9 is

$$\bar{V} = A - bX - cX^2 - dX^3, \tag{2.8.1}$$

where $\bar{V}$ = average variable cost,
X = output,
A, b, c, d = constants.

Although the cubic equation (2.8.1) represents a relatively simple mathematical approach to the approximation of many nonlinear cost

[3] See J. B. Scarborough, *Numerical Mathematical Analysis,* 6th ed., Johns Hopkins Press, Baltimore, 1966, pp. 522–563, for the derivation of empirical formulas.

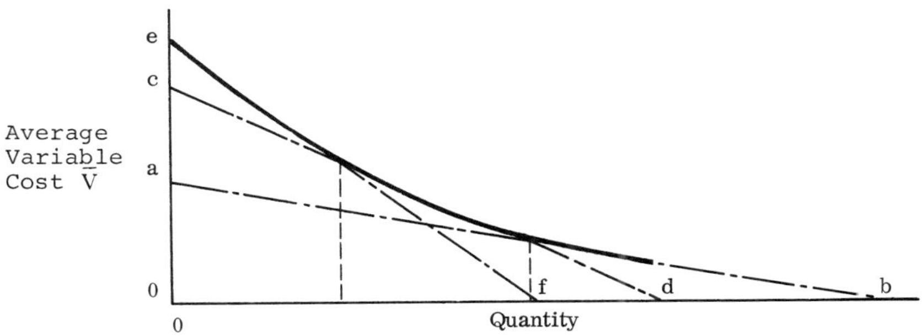

Figure 2.9

functions, it is only one of many mathematical expressions capable of describing such phenomena.[4]

9. COST MODEL AGGREGATION

A system cost model may consist of an aggregation of separate cost models representing the various subsystems in a large scale system. Fig-

[4] *Ibid.*, pp. 554–555.

AGGREGATION OF SUBSYSTEM COST MODELS

PHASE	PHYSICAL FUNCTIONS	COST FUNCTIONS (k)			
	Modules (i) Subsystems (J)	Equipment	Maintenance	Administration	Totals
R&D	#1 Subsystem ⋮ m				Σ ⋮ Σ
	Total R&D	Σ	Σ	Σ	ΣΣ = R
INVESTMENT	#1 Subsystem #1 Module ⋮ l				Σ ⋮ Σ
	Total	Σ	Σ	Σ	ΣΣ
	#2 Subsystem #1 Module ⋮ l				Σ ⋮ Σ
	Total	Σ	Σ	Σ	ΣΣ
	mth Subsystem #1 Module ⋮ l				Σ ⋮ Σ
	Total	Σ	Σ	Σ	ΣΣ
	Total Investment	ΣΣ	ΣΣ	ΣΣ	ΣΣΣ = I
Annual Operation	#1 Subsystem ⋮ m				Σ ⋮ Σ
	Total Operation	Σ	Σ	Σ	ΣΣ
Operation R&D and Invest. All	Total Oper. x(n) Years Total R&D + Investment Total System Cost	nΣ	nΣ	nΣ	nΣ Σ=O R + I R + I + O

Figure 2.10

ure 2.10 illustrates in a matrix format an aggregative type of cost model that contains multiple subsystems. Several major tradeoffs can be conducted with such a model:

1. Tradeoffs may be made within a subsystem between the R & D, the investment, and the annual operation to minimize each subsystem's cost with respect to a given subsystem performance.

2. Tradeoffs may be made within the system between the subsystems to minimize the total system cost with respect to a given over-all performance.

3. Tradeoffs in which a particular subsystem cost is minimized and the increase in the total system cost, if any, is measured.

System cost models of this nature are usually always computer implemented, thereby reducing the manual arithmetic computation to a minimum. It is desirable therefore to convert the matrix format of Figure 2.10 into a mathematical notation that will facilitate the computer programming process, as shown in (2.9.1):

$$
\begin{aligned}
(2.9.1)\quad C = {} & \alpha\Big[\Big(\sum_{i=1}^{l}\sum_{j=1}^{m}\sum_{k=1}^{n} R_m\Big) + \Big(\sum_{i=1}^{l}\sum_{j=1}^{m}\sum_{k=1}^{n} R_l\Big) + \Big(\sum_{i=1}^{l}\sum_{j=1}^{m}\sum_{k=1}^{n} R_c\Big)\Big] \\
& + \beta\Big[\Big(\sum_{i=1}^{l}\sum_{j=1}^{m}\sum_{k=1}^{n} I_m\Big) + \Big(\sum_{i=1}^{l}\sum_{j=1}^{m}\sum_{k=1}^{n} I_l\Big) + \Big(\sum_{i=1}^{l}\sum_{j=1}^{m}\sum_{k=1}^{n} I_c\Big)\Big] \\
& - \gamma\Big[\Big(\sum_{i=1}^{l}\sum_{j=1}^{m}\sum_{k=1}^{n} H_m\Big) + \Big(\sum_{i=1}^{l}\sum_{j=1}^{m}\sum_{k=1}^{n} H_l\Big) + \Big(\sum_{i=1}^{l}\sum_{j=1}^{m}\sum_{k=1}^{n} H_c\Big)\Big] \\
& + \xi\Big[\Big(\sum_{i=1}^{l}\sum_{j=1}^{m}\sum_{k=1}^{n} O_m\Big) + \Big(\sum_{i=1}^{l}\sum_{j=1}^{m}\sum_{k=1}^{n} O_l\Big) + \Big(\sum_{i=1}^{l}\sum_{j=1}^{m}\sum_{k=1}^{n} O_c\Big)\Big] \\
& - \Big[\sum_{i=1}^{l}\sum_{j=1}^{m}\sum_{k=1}^{n} S_{ijk}\Big],
\end{aligned}
$$

where

$\alpha, \beta, \gamma, \xi$ = coefficients of value added (used to raise input values to user cost level),

R = research and development = total cost incurred before production,

I = investment = total cost incurred in production,

O = operation = total cost incurred in use subsequent to production until scrapped,

H = inheritance = total cost saved by utilizing resources made available by and charged to other programs,

S = scrap value = residual value at end of useful life,

m = material,
l = labor,
c = capital,
i = ith module,
j = jth subsystem,
k = kth cost function.

10. DIFFERENTIAL COST MODELS

There are, on occasion, problems in which the system alternatives being considered all make use of an identical resource in the fulfillment of a common objective. An example of such a situation confronted by the author involved a ship-based versus a land-based missile range-tracking radar system. The identical resource in this case was the radar system. Instead of an aggregative-type cost model, a differential cost model was used to simplify the identification of the most economical alternative. With the differential cost model approach the costs associated with the radar system could be essentially ignored (except for the addition of a stable gyro platform reference required aboard the ship.) The only costs measured for each alternative therefore were the ship and its operation versus a land-based building and operation therein. The basic approach is shown graphically in Figure 2.11. Because all of the identical resources have been excluded in a differential cost model, it cannot be used to determine the total system cost to the user but only to indicate the alternative that will be the least costly. By adding to the cost of the least-cost alternative a gross estimate of the identical

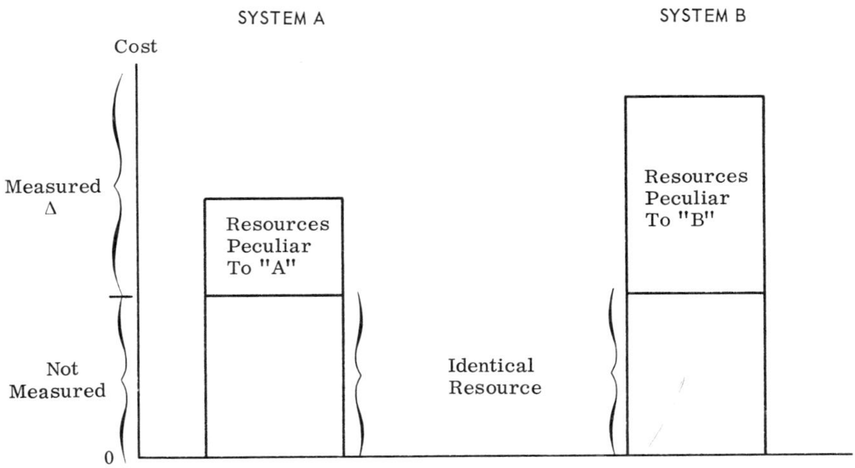

Figure 2.11

resources excluded an indication of the total system cost to the user can be made.

11. PROBABILISTIC COST

It is frequently more meaningful to compare the costs of different systems in terms of a probability of being attained rather than by merely comparing their central tendency values. This is true regardless of whether the comparison model has an aggregative or differential format. The total system cost of an alternative with a low standard deviation may then actually be preferred to an alternative with a lower mean cost but a much higher standard deviation (see Figure 2.12.).

The cost of a system that is not actually in an operational state is rarely practical or possible to determine precisely. The evaluation of the degree of uncertainty surrounding a most probable cost value requires determination of the probability distributions of the various cost elements, not merely their expected or modal values. This requires a method of system cost estimating in which the individual costs are not presented as single points (\$1,000,000) but rather as estimates encompassing probability distributions or at least incorporating extrema (e.g., \$1,000,000 ± \$200,000 with a probability of 0.9 of being in this range). The result of a system cost synthesis made on this basis is not a fixed-point cost but rather a probability distribution of costs. The importance of this approach is seen in Figure 2.12, in which it

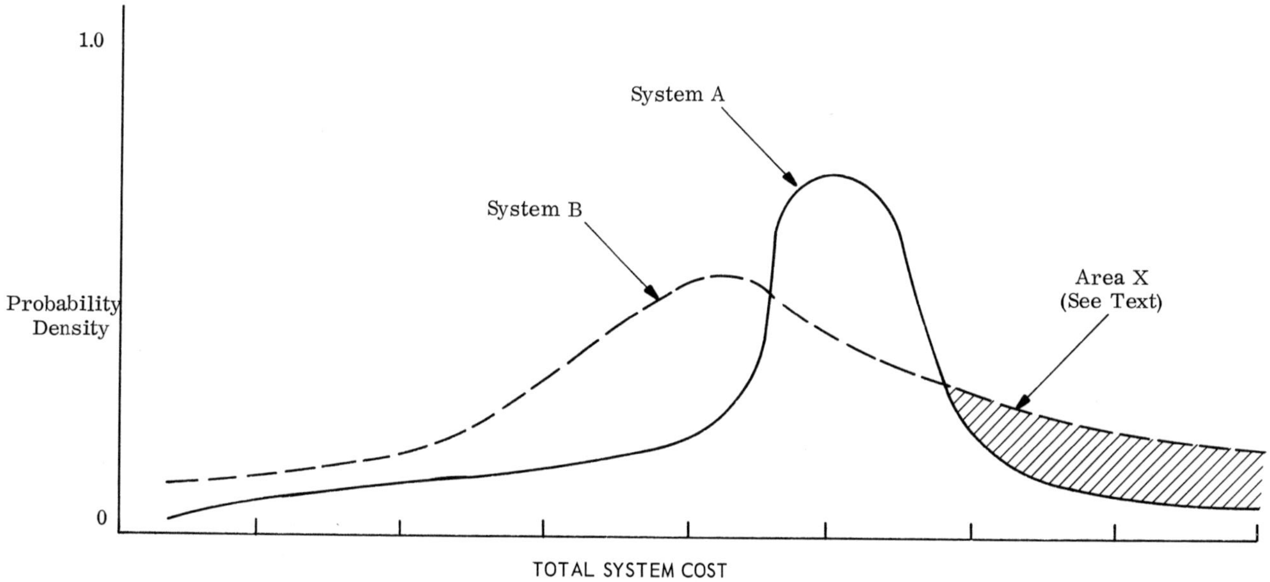
1.0
Probability Density
0
System A
System B
Area X (See Text)
TOTAL SYSTEM COST

Figure 2.12

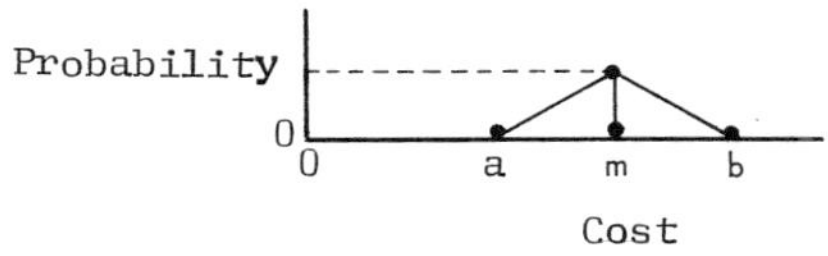

Figure 2.13

may not be possible to determine on the basis of a purely analytic measure the system that is more desirable. What is revealed is the possibility that system B might cost more than system A, as shown by area X.

There are several probability distributions that may be discussed re their suitability to describe cost estimates: the normal probability distribution—this is generally inappropriate because symmetry cannot be arbitrarily assumed; the beta probability distribution—this requires too many parameters to describe the distribution readily; the rectangular probability distribution—this considers only the range and not the most likely value of the estimate; the triangular probability distribution—this is the only one recommended because it requires the least amount of information to give a meaningful description of the cost estimates. A triangular distribution requires only three parameters for each cost: the minimum cost (a), the maximum cost (b), and the most probable cost (m), as shown graphically in Figure 2.13.

With only these three parameters, the expected value $E(c)$ and the variance $V(c)$ of the costs may be computed by using the following equations:

$$(2.11.1) \quad E(c) = \frac{1}{3(b-a)}\left[\frac{m^2(2m-3a)+a^3}{m-a} + \frac{m^2(2m-3b)+b^3}{b-m}\right],$$

$$(2.11.2) \quad V(c) = E(c^2) - [E(c)]^2.$$

For computational ease the individual cost estimates may be linearly transformed to a 0–1 scale. Thus a distribution with parameters

$$a = \$100{,}000,$$
$$m = \$300{,}000,$$
$$b = \$400{,}000$$

would be transformed to $a = 0$, $m = \frac{2}{3}$, and $b = 1$. After computing the mean and the variance these values are then transformed to the initial scale.

Costs that are known with certainty or costs in which only one point estimate can be obtained are degenerate cases and have $a = m = b = c$, and variance $= 0$.

Costs for which only a range of values can be obtained are assumed to have a most likely value, $m = (b + a)/2$.

The central limit theorem[5] establishes the conditions under which the sum of mutually independent random variables with a common distribution will be asymptotically normally distributed with a mean of

$$E(C) = \sum_{i=1}^{n} E(c_i), \tag{2.11.3}$$

where $E(c_i)$ = expected value of ith cost component and a variance of

$$V(C) = \sum_{i=1}^{n} E(c_i^2) - [E(c_i)]^2, \tag{2.11.4}$$

from which the distribution of the total system cost may be obtained.

Probabilistic Matrices

Referring back to Figure 2.1, there can be derived, for each alternative system, a probability matrix version of Figure 2.1 in which the point value for each cell is replaced by a triangular probability distribution. This matrix will then provide the following:

1. A probabilistic prediction of the costs to be incurred by physical function (sum of line triangular distributions).
2. A probabilistic prediction of the costs to be incurred by cost function (sum of column triangular distributions).
3. A probabilistic prediction of the total system cost (sum of either the line or column sums).

Extensions of the Probability Model

One of the more desirable extensions of the model would be the use of conditional probability distributions for related costs; for example, the cost of the spare parts for the year (n) may be very much a function of the maintenance cost for the year $(n - 1)$. An effective way to handle such an extension would be to make a Monte Carlo simulation of all the elements in the system.[6] The Monte Carlo technique then, in effect, constructs through the means of computer calculations the many possible

[5] William Feller, *An Introduction to Probability Theory and Its Applications,* Vol. II, Wiley, New York, 1966, pp. 252–259.

[6] See Gerald J. Hahn and Samuel S. Shapiro, *Statistical Models in Engineering,* Wiley, New York, 1967, pp. 236–252.

conditional combinations of randomly varying element costs, thereby obtaining the distribution of the total system cost. A second desirable extension would be a relaxation of the triangular distribution requirement. For many cost estimates a distribution might be used which more accurately describes the real cost distribution.

In a system cost-effectiveness analysis the companion model to the cost model is, of course, the effectiveness model which is the subject matter of Part III, next.

SUGGESTED READINGS

- Large, Joseph P. *Concepts and Procedures of Cost Analysis,* RM-3589-PR. The RAND Corporation, June 1963. A comprehensive view of military cost analysis with particular emphasis on cost estimating relationships.
- Novick, David. *System and Total Force Cost Analysis,* RM-2695-PR. The RAND Corporation, April 1961. One of the original studies in systems cost analysis.
- Parzen, Emanuel. *Modern Probability Theory and Its Applications.* Wiley, New York, 1960. A basic text in probability theory for the mathematically oriented reader.
- Scarborough, James B. *Numerical Mathematical Analysis,* 6th ed. Johns Hopkins Press, Baltimore, 1966. An outstanding textbook in the application of mathematics to numerical results.

General Notation Used in Part III

E = total system effectiveness
$E(E)$ = expected value of total system effectiveness
$E(P)$ = expected performance of system
$E(A)$ = expected availability of system
$E(R)$ = expected reliability of system
$E(S)$ = expected survivability of system
C = confidence

Part III

SYSTEM EFFECTIVENESS MODELS

The objective in Part III is to develop the structure of system effectiveness models. These models will be particularly adapted to the measurement of the expected value of total system effectiveness in cost-effectiveness analyses. The system effectiveness model should faithfully represent the effectiveness analog of all the elements of a system, just as the cost model should represent the cost analog of the system. The definition of the system's elements depends on the level of use (as discussed in Part I), which then concomitantly fixes the effectiveness level as well as the costing level. The output of a system effectiveness model is the result of a derating or factoring procedure. This output may be either a single expected value or a frequency distribution of values representing the probability density function of system effectiveness.

1. PROBABILITY PRODUCT MODEL

Perhaps the single most distinguishing characteristic of system effectiveness models in comparison to system cost models is in the mathematical operations involved; the effectiveness model consists principally of a series of multiplications, whereas the cost model consists principally of a series of summations. Another fundamental differentiating characteristic is the continuity of the dependent variable over the system lifetime, effectiveness being essentially a discontinuous function of time, whereas cost is continually accumulated until the system is scrapped. Although other distinguishing characteristics could be cited, they are, in general, either trivial and/or essentially not germane to this discussion.

The initial phase in system effectiveness model development is the assembly of the appropriate elements of effectiveness into two design-oriented classifications, since the discipline of an effectiveness model consists in essence of the interaction between these two design concepts:

1. The basic design—a parametric description of a virgin system as it would exist and operate in the absence of adverse influences.

2. The realized design—a parametric description of the virgin system after being derated by its operation in the planned environment.

An over-all expression that describes the interaction between these two design concepts is

$$E(E) = [E(P)C_p][E(A)C_a][E(R)C_r][E(S)C_s], \tag{3.1.1}$$

where $E(E) = \bar{E}$ = expected effectiveness of system,
$E(P) = \bar{P}$ = expected performance of system (the basic design),
C_p = statistical confidence in performance.

$$E(A) = \bar{A} = \text{expected availability of system}, \tag{3.1.2}$$

which in the limit

$$= \frac{E(U)}{[E(U) + E(D)]} = \frac{\bar{U}}{(\bar{U} + \bar{D})},$$

where $\bar{U}$ = mean uptime = mean time between failure,
$\bar{D}$ = mean downtime = mean corrective maintenance downtime, including supply downtime and administrative downtime,

C_a = statistical confidence in availability.

$$E(R) = \bar{R} = \text{expected reliability of system} \tag{3.1.3}$$

$$= 1 - P_f,$$

where P_f = probability of failure,
C_r = statistical confidence in reliability.

$$E(S) = \bar{S} = \text{expected survivability of system} \tag{3.1 4}$$

$$= 1 - P_k,$$

where P_k = probability of kill,
C_s = statistical confidence in survivability.

Equation 3.1.1 is based on the combinatorial product rule from probability theory for events occurring either in sequence or simultaneously. This equation represents only the basic case in which each of the parameters is given an equal weighting in determining the over-all effectiveness of the system. The expected effectiveness of the system $E(E)$ is not necessarily optimal at this stage, since the marginal return of each of the parameters with respect to the total effectiveness has not been equalized. Each of the parameters in (3.1.1) is now described in greater detail.

2. BASIC PERFORMANCE

The basic performance variable $E(P)$ in (3.1.1) represents the expected value of a distribution of possible performance values that would fall within given statistical confidence limits. Graphically, the basic performance variable and the confidence limits associated therewith might appear as shown in Figure 3.1. The shaded areas represent the performance values to be expected in (100 percent—the confidence percent chosen) cases; for example, if the 95 percent confidence limits had been chosen, this would mean that those limits would be exceeded five times in 100. Since there are statistical confidence limits associated with each parameter in (3.1.1), a description of confidence limits and the procedure used to derive them is given next.

Confidence Limits

The statistical confidence level is a measure of the expectancy that a sample interval will contain the true value of the population parameter. The interval, which is estimated to contain the true value, is known as the confidence interval, and the interval end points are better known as the confidence limits.

The confidence or fiducial variable is based on the concept of a probability distribution around a sample mean.[1] The customary procedure for deriving statistical confidence limits is as follows:

1. Select, a priori, a confidence level in percent ($C = 0 \rightarrow 100$) which, in effect, asks you to state your tolerance for values beyond the limits

[1] F. E. Croxton and D. J. Cowden, *Applied General Statistics,* 2nd ed., Prentice-Hall, Englewood Cliffs, N.J., 1955, pp. 648–650.

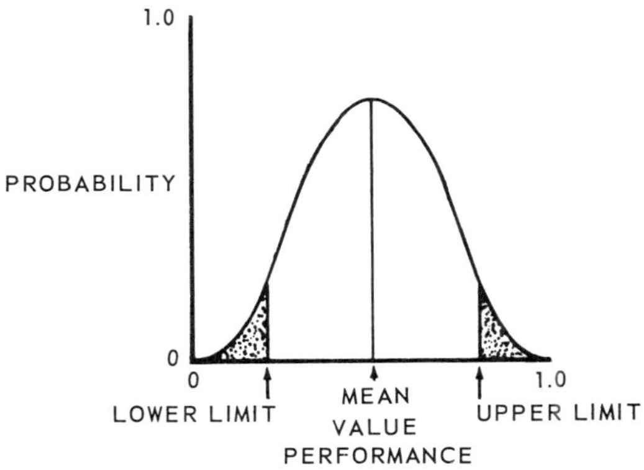

Figure 3.1

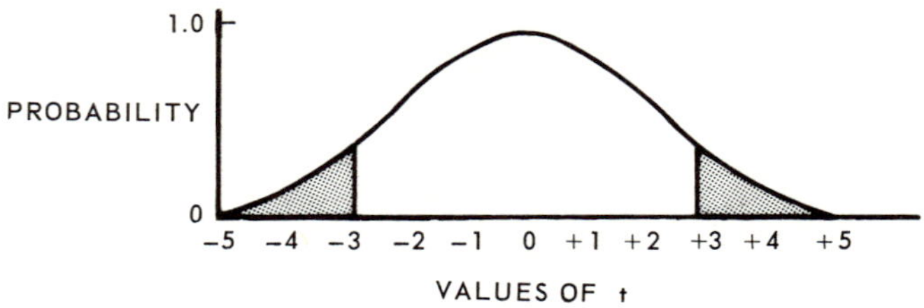

Figure 3.2

to be established. Since most system designs are based on a philosophy of integrity, the confidence levels chosen are usually at least 90 percent.

2. Determine the limits within which the ith effectiveness parameter can be expected to fall with the degree of confidence chosen. Both limit values may be derived from the following expression.[2]

$$\bar{X}_p = \bar{X} \pm t\hat{\sigma}_{\bar{x}}, \tag{3.2.1}$$

where $\bar{X}_p$ = the arithmetic mean of the ith effectiveness parameter (population),

$\bar{X}$ = the arithmetic mean of the ith effectiveness parameter (sample),

t = the value of the shaded areas of the t distribution (see Figure 3.2), obtained by entering the t table[3] with the number of degrees of freedom and the selected confidence level; the number of degrees of freedom n is given by $n = N - 1$, where N = the number of items in the sample,

$\hat{\sigma}_{\bar{x}}$ = the estimated (signified by the cap ^) standard error[4] of $\bar{X} = \sqrt{\Sigma x^2/N}$, where x = deviation of the sample from the $\bar{X}$.

The interpretation of (3.2.1) is, "that there is an uncertainty that the mean of the population falls within the limits derived, but there is a stated confidence percentage that it does so."

3. If the limits within which the ith effectiveness parameter can be expected to fall (with the degree of confidence chosen) are acceptable, derate the ith effectiveness parameter by the confidence percent.

[2] *Ibid.*
[3] Ibid., pp. 750–751.
[4] Ibid., pp. 215–217.

Multiple Performance Parameters

Frequently, a system will be characterized by more than one basic performance parameter and the expected value of P in (3.1.1) may have to represent an index of a combination of expected basic performances of various subsystems.[5] The simplest index may be derived by imagining either a system with subsystems whose performances are binary or a system with more than one binary performance parameter. The manner in which the index of expected over-all performance $E(P)$ would vary as the subsystems, or performance parameters, catastrophically degrade is shown in Table 3.1 for hypothetical system ALPHA. In this table

Table 3.1
ALPHA System

Index of Expected Over-all System Performance $E(P)$	Total Number of Subsystems or Performance Parameters "Full On"	Subsystems or Performance Parameters Expected Percent "On"	
		A	B
100	2	100	100
50	1	100	0
0	0	0	0

the first column may be considered as a function of either the second or third column, since both indicate, in effect, binary on-off type information. Any fault whatsoever in either of the subsystems or with either of the performance parameters in the ALPHA system will immediately reduce the index of expected over-all system performance by 50 percent. By employing subsystems, or performance parameters, that degrade "gracefully"[6] instead of catastrophically the over-all effect on system performance of a single failure can be sharply reduced, as may be seen in Table 3.2 for hypothetical system BETA.

In this table for the BETA system and in the subsequent table for the GAMMA system the first column is truly only a function of the third column, the center column merely indicating a binary on-off type summary of the third column.

[5] The term *basic performance* is assumed throughout the remainder of this section wherever the word performance is used.

[6] Graceful degradation is not a system characteristic obtainable only with systems containing multiple subsystems or multiple performance parameters but is introduced under this heading merely because many simple nonredundant systems generally have this feature as a natural advantage.

Table 3.2
BETA System

Index of Expected Over-all System Performance $E(P)$	Total Number of Subsystems or Performance Parameters "On"	Subsystems or Performance Parameters Expected Percent "On"	
		A	*B*
100	2	100	100
90	2	90	90
80	2	80	80
70	2	70	70
60	2	60	60
50	2	50	50
40	2	40	40
30	2	30	30
20	2	20	20
10	2	10	10
0	0	0	0

Table 3.3
GAMMA System

Index of Expected Over-all System Performance $E(P)$	Total Number of Subsystems or Performance Parameters "On"	Subsystems or Performance Parameters Expected Percent "On"	
		Duplexed (Parallel Redundancy)	
		A	*B*
100	4	100	100
100	4	90	90
100	4	80	80
100	4	70	70
100	4	60	60
100	4	50	50
80	2	40	40
60	2	30	30
40	2	20	20
20	2	10	10
0	0	0	0

The BETA system may be described as a balanced system which degrades "gracefully" in proportion to the degree of subsystem, or performance parameter, degradation. By incorporating redundancy in the system full over-all system performance may be maintained up to the limit of redundancy as shown in Table 3.3 for hypothetical system GAMMA.

The difference in the design philosophies between the BETA and GAMMA systems is summarized in the schematic diagram of Figure 3.3. The BETA system's performance is always directly proportional to the combined subsystems performance, so that when both subsystems are operating at 50 percent of capacity, for example, the over-all performance is also at 50 percent of capacity. The GAMMA system degrades

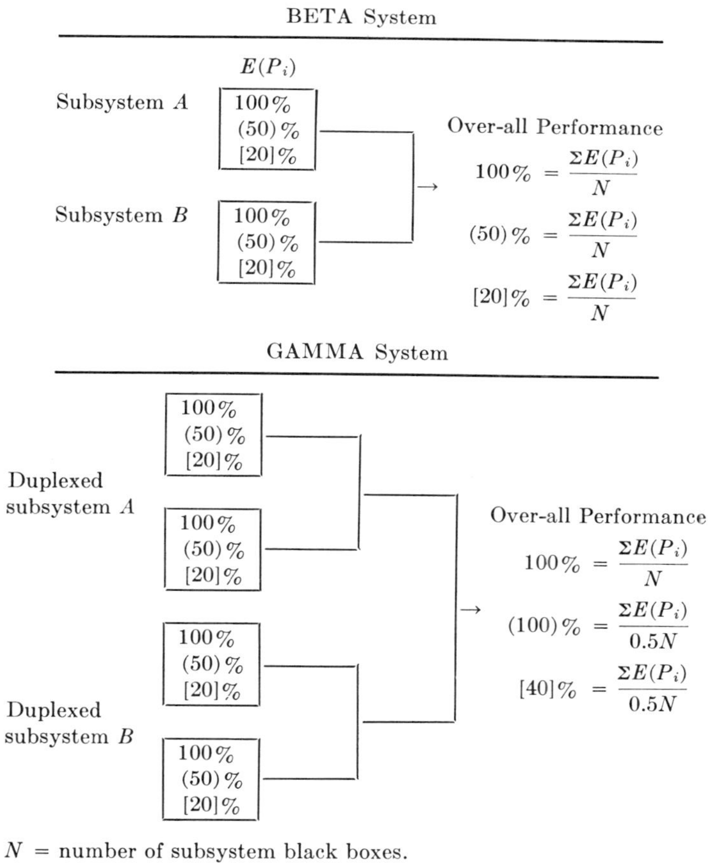

Figure 3.3

by permitting both subsystems to decrease to 50 percent of capacity before the over-all performance is affected. In effect, the GAMMA system achieves an in-depth reliability through the use of redundancy.

Obviously many mathematical variations of these basic system configurations are possible. The purpose here has been merely to introduce the reader to the fundamentals of measuring the over-all performance of systems that may contain multiple subsystems or may have multiple performance parameters. A more generalized but somewhat more mathematical discussion of performance measurement may be found later in Section 6 on model expansion.

3. AVAILABILITY

Systems that can be maintained may be generally rated in terms of the fraction of time that they are available to perform their mission, their unavailability being due to whatever maintenance may be required from time to time. As such, availability is a basic performance derating parameter of the maintained system. The appropriate measure of the availability of a maintained system may take different forms, depending on whether the system is to be operated continuously, on a cyclical basis, or randomly as in Table 3.4.[7]

Another term sometimes used for instantaneous availability is operational availability which may be defined as the conditional probability that an equipment in an actual supply environment will be operable at any time t, given that it was operable at time t_0, where $t_0 < t$.[8]

[7] Gerald H. Sandler, *System Reliability Engineering,* Prentice-Hall, Englewood Cliffs, N. J., 1963, pp. 12, 13.

[8] See A. S. Goldman and T. B. Slattery, *Maintainability: A Major Element of System Effectiveness,* Wiley, New York, 1964, p. 26.

Table 3.4

Mode of System Operation	Appropriate Measure of Availability
Continuous	Steady-state availability: the proportion of time that the system is available for use when the time interval considered is very large.
Cyclical	Average uptime: the proportion of time within a specified interval (O, T) that the system is available for use.
Random	Instantaneous availability: the probability that the system will be available at any random time t.

Since in the limit the average uptime and the instantaneous availability will approach the steady-state availability, the expected availability of a maintained system $E(A)$ was defined in (3.1.2) as $\bar{A} = \bar{U}/(\bar{U} + \bar{D})$. In those cases in which the system has two or more subsystems the measurement of the over-all system availability becomes a function not only of the mode of system operation but also of the individual subsystems $\bar{U}$ and $\bar{D}$ and the manner in which the system is configured (subsystems in series and/or parallel). The mean subsystem uptimes and downtimes, assuming a system of subsystems consisting of identical units, would be

$$\bar{U}_j = \frac{1}{n} \sum_{i=1}^{n} U_i, \tag{3.3.1}$$

where $\bar{U}_j$ = mean time between failure in the jth subsystem,
U_i = mean time between failure in the ith unit of the jth subsystem,
n = number of units.

$$\bar{D}_j = \frac{1}{n} \sum_{i=1}^{n} D_i, \tag{3.3.2}$$

where $\bar{D}_j$ = mean downtime in the jth subsystem,
D_i = mean downtime in the ith unit of the jth subsystem.

The $\bar{U}$ and $\bar{D}$ are both complex functions of the integrity built into a system or subsystem as well as the integrity of the maintenance provided. For systems with a low duty cycle, such that the idle time is much greater than the usage time, it is expected that the availability would approach unity, since nearly all failures can be repaired while the system is idle and therefore not counted as downtime.[9] Since no general expression can be given to fit the many possible variations in system configuration and operation, it is felt that the reader would benefit more by consulting the cited references rather than attempt to develop such material here.

For new systems on which no failure or repair history is available there are several possible alternatives:

1. Construct a physical prototype of the system and subject it to an accelerated environmental stress.

2. Construct a mathematical analog of the system and subject it to an environmental stress in an accelerated time frame by using a computer-simulation technique.

[9] Sandler, *op. cit.*, p. 13.

Many excellent references are available on the subject of simulation. The text by Naylor et al., cited at the end of Part III, is basic for those readers who would like to develop a working knowledge of simulation techniques.

Assuming that a system has incurred a failure and the defective component has been identified, there is the question whether to repair the component at the operational level, discard it and replace it with a new component, or replace it with a new component and ship the defective unit back to a repair depot. Each of these alternatives has a different cost associated with it and each in turn will have different effects on the over-all system's effectiveness.[10] In making the decision between these alternatives, the cost of repair either at the operational level or the depot must take into account the degree of serviceability designed into the failed component as well as the technical skill of the maintenance manpower available. Obviously an adequate in-depth consideration of the availability parameter is a necessary and often critical factor in the measurement of total system effectiveness.

4. RELIABILITY

The expected reliability $E(R)$ is defined basically in (3.1.3) as $\bar{R} = (1 - P_f)$, the probability of failure. Reliability and availability are often confused concepts, but for the purpose of this discussion reliability is defined as the probability that a system will perform as expected for the duration of its mission, given that the system was initially in the "go" state. For a system with a high duty cycle, in which the mean idle time is much less than the mean usage time, the mean repair time must be kept much less than the mean idle time or repairs will not be able to be made without significantly decreasing system availability.

In a system with a multiple mission function the expected reliability becomes

$$E(R) = \lim 1 - \frac{N_f}{N_m}, \qquad N_m \rightarrow \infty, \tag{3.4.1}$$

where N_f = number of missions failed,
N_m = number of missions.

The term failure used in both the operational availability and mission reliability measures refers to a complete failure. The cases for a partial failure for either operational availability or mission reliability are more complex and require the introduction of the notion of a degraded system

[10] Goldman and Slattery, *op. cit.*, p. 21.

performance, as described earlier under "Multiple Performance Parameters." Systems may be broadly classified for this purpose according to their sensitivity to subsystem outages. The differences between graceful, "normal," and catastrophic degradation may be seen by examining Figure 3.4. Systems whose subsystems are configured serially (like the chain) will, of course, degrade catastrophically. By using parallel (redundant) subsystems the over-all system performance may be made to degrade more gracefully. There is a min. cost, generally, between incorporating more and more redundancy versus the cost of equipment downtime as shown in Figure 3.5. There is, furthermore, the problem of optimally allocating redundancy among the subsystems in a large-scale system such that the marginal contributions to system *uptime* are equalized. It is apparent from Figure 3.5 that the amount of redundancy that minimizes total system cost is not the amount of redundancy that minimizes total system downtime. The appropriate degree of balance between these two design goal extremes should be dictated by the matching of the criteria to the system's mission requirements.

Another consideration in system reliability design is the difference in approach required between nonmaintained systems (e.g., satellites) and maintained systems. Since no maintenance is feasible or permissible in a nonmaintained system (by definition), the system integrity becomes strongly dependent on the degree of reliability achievable. The basic

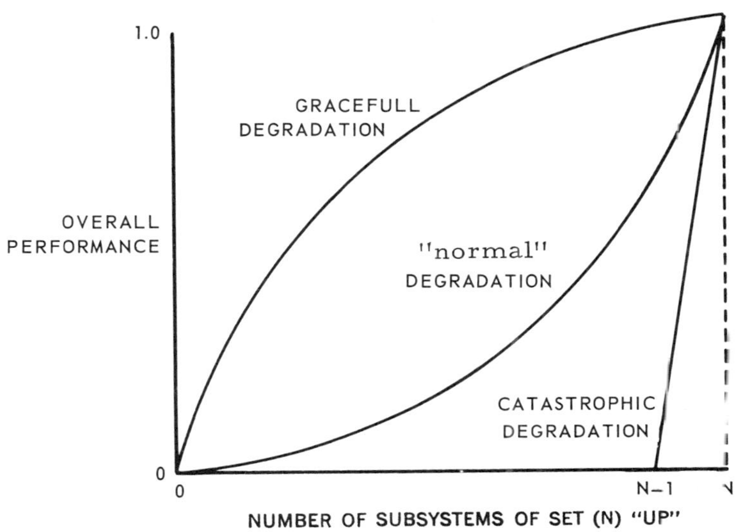

Figure 3.4

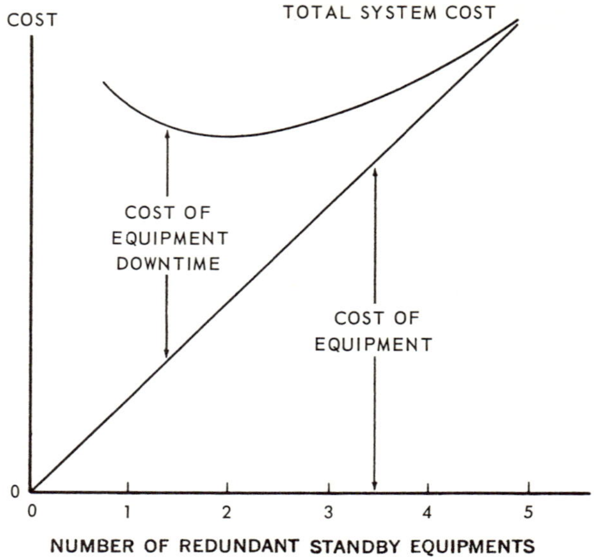

Figure 3.5

tradeoff then in a nonmaintained system is the cost of system reliability versus the cost of system replacement. Systems that can be maintained, however, may tradeoff the cost of system maintainability versus the cost of system reliability as long as the sum of the two is less than the cost of system replacement.

It is not the intent here to develop the design criteria for the optimization of system reliability any further, the main purpose having been to introduce the reader to the major reliability considerations involved in system cost-effectiveness analyses. The Sandler reference is recommended for those readers who desire additional background in this subject.

5. SURVIVABILITY

In (3.1.4) the expected survivability $E(S)$ was defined as $\bar{S} = (1 - P_k)$, the probability of kill, which is customarily used in weapon-system effectiveness analyses. There are, however, commercial analogs of P_k; for example, survivability threatened by technological obsolescence or patent infringement. Regardless of whether the system is military or commercial, the derivation of system survivability is usually a complex function of many variables. The two basic approaches to a survivability analysis are the following:

Microanalysis

The weapon-system survivability problem may be microanalyzed in terms of an expected error in being hit with a single shot (known better as the miss distance[11]) and the capability of the target to withstand smaller and smaller miss distances (known as the hardness).

The functional relationship between the probability of kill, the miss distance, and the hardness is shown in Figure 3.6, in which, as the overpressure resistance (hardness) is reduced to zero (atmospheric pressure), the miss distance increases. Since the specific functional relationships between the variables in Figure 3.6 are not germane to the discussion, they may be written simply as

$$(3.5.1) \qquad P_k = f\left(\frac{1}{D} \exp p\right).$$

The miss distance D, if measured merely in terms of the range R, may be expressed as the sum of the partial derivatives of range with respect to all the range sensitive parameters, times the respective range parametric deviations

$$(3.5.2) \qquad \Delta R = \frac{\partial R}{\partial V}\,\Delta V + \frac{\partial R}{\partial W}\,\Delta W + \cdots,$$

where, for example, V = muzzle velocity of the projectile,
W = projectile weight.

[11] For the purpose of this discussion miss distance is considered to be a simple measurement of the rectilinear distance between two points in space.

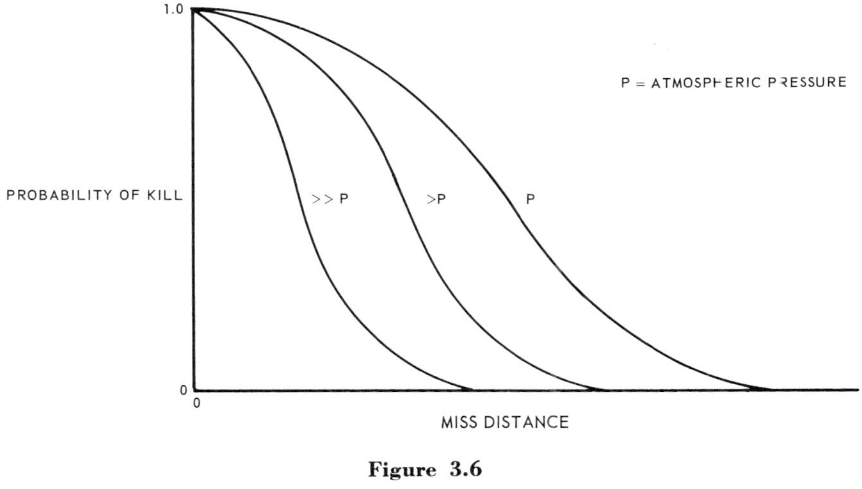

Figure 3.6

A more comprehensive method of analyzing the survivability of a weapon system is to use first a microanalysis to determine the individual weapon survivability and then to integrate the effect of a multitude of these weapons in a macroanalysis of opposing forces.

Macroanalysis

In 1916 in London Frederick William Lanchester formulated his now well-known set of Lanchester equations describing the relative attrition of units of opposing forces.[12] Although the original formulations by Lanchester are restricted in utility, they nonetheless have been the foundation for much additional research and are described here mainly for their tutorial value. These are differential equations that describe for each combat the rates of change with time (T) in the numbers of opposing forces (m and n) in terms of an exchange ratio (E):

$$\frac{dm}{dT} = -\frac{1}{1+E}, \tag{3.5.3}$$

$$\frac{dn}{dT} = -\frac{E}{1+E}, \tag{3.5.4}$$

where[13]

$$m = m_0 - \frac{T}{1+E}, \tag{3.5.5}$$

$$n = n_0 - \frac{TE}{1+E}, \tag{3.5.6}$$

and

$$E = \frac{dn}{dm}, \tag{3.5.7}$$

resulting in

$$n_0 - n = E(m_0 - m), \tag{3.5.8}$$

where m = number of combatants in the red force at any instant,
n = number of combatants in the blue force at any instant,
T = time in terms of number of combats,
E = the exchange rate that equals the ratio between the average number of blue combatants lost to the average number of red combatants lost.

[12] See Philip M. Morse and George E. Kimball, *Methods of Operations Research,* 1st ed. rev., published jointly by the M.I.T. Technology Press and Wiley, New York, 1951, pp. 63–77.

[13] The m and n zero subscript refer to the original force numbers.

Since these are linear equations, the set is referred to at times as Lanchester's linear law.[14] The superiority of one force or the other, in weapons or training, is reflected in the exchange rate. The powerful simplicity of these equations is obvious, and for the purpose of deriving a measure of survivability for inclusion in (3.1.1) they are directly applicable.

6. MODEL EXPANSION

The system effectiveness model developed so far could, of course, be used in a hand-type solution of relatively simple systems. Similar to the expansion of the cost model, the effectiveness model also is becoming an increasingly complex entity. Two principal forces at work are escalating these models to higher and higher numbers of parameters. First, the systems being analyzed are growing in complexity and, second, the rapid evolution of machine data processing has made feasible the implementation of complex models, before which hand solutions would have

Table 3.5

Partial Derivatives		Normalization Constant		Weights W
$\partial P/\partial P_i = 2.75$	×	0.25	=	0.6875
$\partial P/\partial P_j = 1.00$	×	0.25	=	0.2500
$\partial P/\partial P_k = 0.25$	×	0.25	=	0.0625
$\Sigma = 4.00$	×	0.25	=	1.0000

P = system performance.
$P_{i,j,k}$ = subsystem performance.

been impractical. It is of interest therefore to expand the foregoing basic equation (3.1.1) into an expression that will include a weighting factor rationale for combining in one over-all index the many subsystems and performance parameters of large-scale systems. In developing such a model, a criterion for the assignment of weights is needed which can be based on a measurement of the "parts" contribution to the performance of the "whole" system. The derivation of the weights in many weighting schemes is often based on deceptively simple premises. It is at this stage in a systems cost-effectiveness analysis in which many undefendable assumptions may be created. This is frequently the result when care is not taken to ascertain the sensitivity of the system's performance to the functioning of its various constituents. The ideal sensi-

[14] *Ibid.*

tivity analysis, assuming zero variance, would consist of deriving the partial derivatives of each subsystem's performance to the over-all performance of the system, as shown in Table 3.5.

The weights W may now be introduced into (3.1.1) as factors resulting in

$$(3.6.1) \qquad E(E) = \left[\frac{\Sigma W_i E(P_i) C_{Pi}}{\Sigma W_i}\right]\left[\frac{\Sigma W_i E(A_i) C_{Ai}}{\Sigma W_i}\right]$$

$$= \left[\frac{\Sigma W_i E(R_i) C_{Ri}}{\Sigma W_i}\right]\left[\frac{\Sigma W_i E(S_i) C_{Si}}{\Sigma W_i}\right],$$

where C_{Pi}, C_{Ai}, C_{Ri}, C_{Si} = confidence in the ith subsystem's performance, availability, reliability, and survivability, respectively.

Equation 3.6.1 may be approximated by

$$(3.6.2) \qquad E(E) = \frac{\Sigma W_i E(P_i) C_{Pi} \cdot E(A_i) C_{Ai} \cdot E(R_i) C_{Ri} \cdot E(S_i) C_{Si}}{\Sigma W_i}.$$

Equation 3.6.2 would be very suitable for systems of the BETA and GAMMA type described earlier.

For multiple performance parameter subsystems, in which each parameter contributes a simple proportionate share to the over-all subsystem performance, (3.6.2) may be expanded simply as

$$(3.6.3) \qquad E(E) = \frac{\Sigma W_i \left[\frac{1}{j} \sum_{i=1}^{j} E(P_{ij})\right] C_{Pi} \cdot E(A_i) C_{Ai} \cdot E(R_i) C_{Ri} \cdot E(S_i) C_{Si}}{\Sigma W_i}$$

where j = number of performance parameters in the ith subsystem.

Another method of introducing the weights is to make them exponents as shown in (3.6.4):

$$(3.6.4) \qquad E(E) = \prod_{i=1}^{n} (E_i C_i)^{W_i},$$

where E_i = ith effectiveness variable,
C_i = confidence in ith effectiveness variable,
W_i = weighting factor expressing relative importance of the E_i,
n = number of effectiveness variables.

7. MAXIMIZING TOTAL SYSTEM EFFECTIVENESS

Just as it was desirable to minimize total system cost while holding effectiveness constant, so it is desirable to maximize total system effectiveness, holding the previously attained minimum cost constant. This is nothing more than the min-max concept developed in the theory of games,[15] discussed in Part IV.

Total system effectiveness may often be increased by adjusting the balance between the various factors of performance, availability, reliability, and survivability; for example, an increase in the weight of a military aircraft's payload may be achieved by reducing or eliminating the weight of its protective shielding against enemy fire; however, the combat survivability of such an aircraft in reaching its target would be lowered. The specific function to be maximized in this example might be the expected deliverable tonnage on target. The combination of aircraft payload weight and shielding weight (assuming that they were the only two sensitive parameters) that resulted in the greatest deliverable tonnage on target would then be optimum.

The maximization of total system effectiveness involves finding the maximizing values of the four independent variables in (3.1.1). The calculus approach to a multivariable optimization is to setup the first-order partial derivatives of each of the variables with respect to the function being maximized (effectiveness).

Since $E = f(P, A, R, S)$ from (3.1.1), if E is to be maximized, the following relationships must be existent:

(3.7.1) $$\frac{\partial E}{\partial P} = 0,$$

(3.7.2) $$\frac{\partial E}{\partial A} = 0,$$

(3.7.3) $$\frac{\partial E}{\partial R} = 0,$$

(3.7.4) $$\frac{\partial E}{\partial S} = 0.$$

Equations 3.7.1 through 3.7.4, when solved simultaneously for the various values of the unknowns, will yield the maximum value for E (if the appropriate second-order conditions are satisfied). The reason for the

[15] John von Neumann and Oskar Morgenstern, *Theory of Games and Economic Behavior,* 3rd ed., Princeton University Press, Princeton, N. J., 1953.

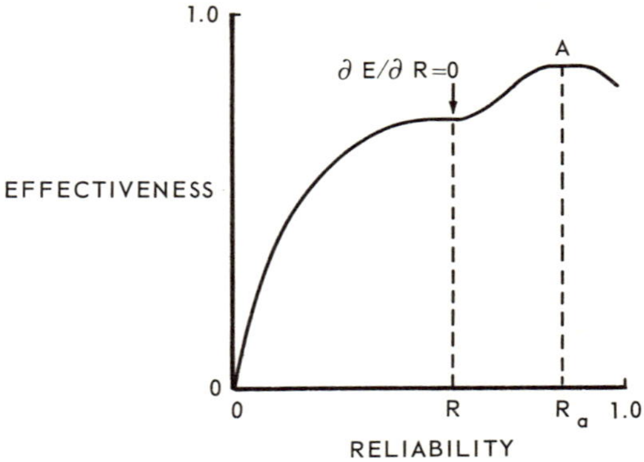

Figure 3.7

second-order condition is to avoid the dilemma associated with a function of one of the variables, for example reliability, which is monotonically increasing but which contains a flat somewhere along the path, as shown in Figure 3.7.

The first derivative maximization condition $\partial E/\partial R$ assures only the existence of a level stretch on the effectiveness hill and in no way indicates the real crest A of the hill. By using the second-order condition $\partial^2 E/\partial R^2$ the true crest A of the hill may be identified, for E will have stopped increasing and if R were increased any further E would begin to decrease. The second-order condition refers to the behavior of the first-order curve $\partial E/\partial R$, as shown in Figure 3.8. With reference to this figure,

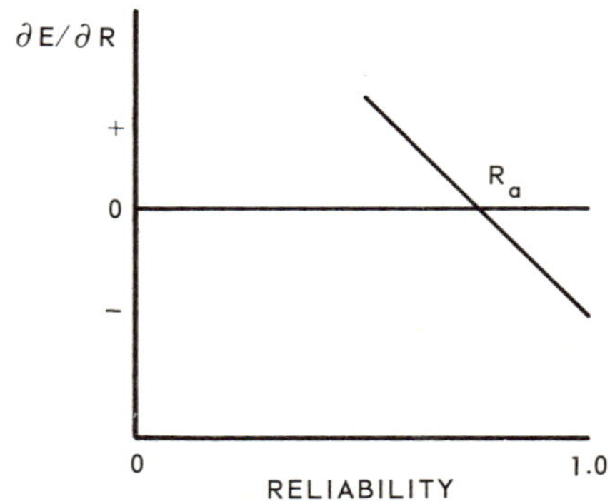

Figure 3.8

the first-order condition required that the curve cut the horizontal axis ($\partial E/\partial R = 0$) at the E-maximizing value of R_a. The second-order condition requires that the slope of the curve at that point R_a be negative, thereby making $\partial E/\partial R$ positive to the left of R_a and negative to the right of R_a. The E maximizing value R_a is thus uniquely defined. Although all of the discussion in this section has concerned the maximization of E, the same procedure could be used to minimize the total system cost by merely requiring that the second derivative be positive.[16]

Although the foregoing discussion may appear to have presented a rather straightforward approach to optimizations in many variables, the reader is cautioned that the approach described assumes ideal experimental conditions. Some of the problems that may be encountered, which will render the application of the basic optimization procedure aforedescribed either more difficult or impossible, are listed here as warning signs.

1. Variables with discontinuities or sharp kinks, the derivatives of which are impossible to impute.

[16] Mathematically, these conditions are not strictly inviolable, for if the second derivative is zero but the fourth is negative the point R_a may still be a maximum and, where the fourth derivative is positive, the point R_a may still be a minimum. Similarly, when the second and fourth derivatives are zero but the sixth is not, the same identifications will ensue, and so the process can continue *ad infinitum*.

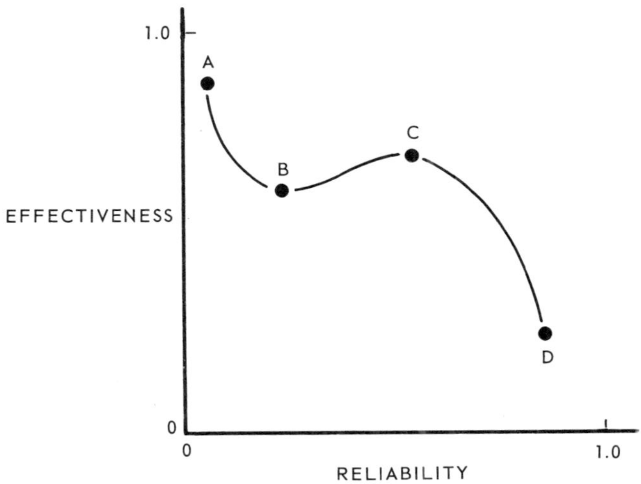

Figure 3.9

2. Variables whose limited range of values preclude the attainment of a true optimum. In such cases the application of mathematical programming (discussed in Chapter 4) is called for.

3. Cases in which the variable may have higher or lower values than a local maximum or minimum, respectively (see Figure 3.9).

4. Cases that are multimodal.

Note in Figure 3.9 that point A is higher than the local maximum of point C and that point D is lower than the local minimum of point B; however, neither point A nor D defines a maximum or minimum hill. The foregoing differential calculus will also not work when there is more than one local maxima or minima, in which case the technique of "broad-jump" hunting (integer programming discussed in Chapter 4) will provide a global identification within the range of the broadest jump in the independent variable.

8. PERIOD VERSUS MISSION EFFECTIVENESS

In Part II on system cost models period costing was described as a method of making cost comparisons of alternative systems within the same time frame. Similarly, the effectiveness of alternative systems may be compared within a common time frame; however, the effectiveness comparison time frame (shaded area) will always be a shorter interval than the cost comparison time frame shown in Figure 3.10. Note within the effectiveness time frame that the over-all effectiveness trend through-

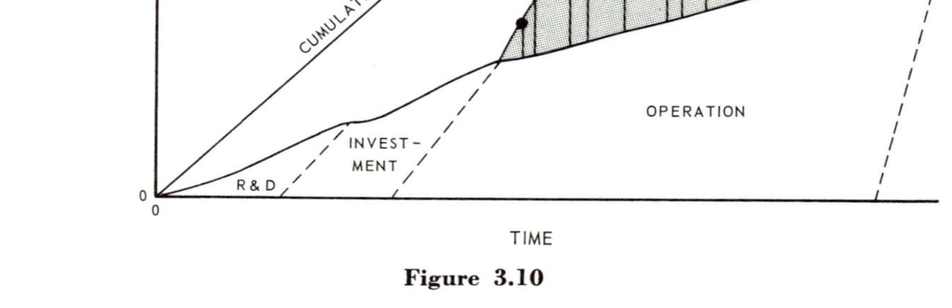

Figure 3.10

out the operational period of the system represents a mathematical averaging of the discrete mission averages, which may be expressed most simply as

$$E(E) = \bar{E} = \frac{1}{n}\sum_{i=1}^{n} \bar{E}_i, \tag{3.8.1}$$

where $\bar{E}_i$ = mean value of ith mission effectiveness,
n = number of missions.

In the case in which the system is to operate in more than one mode simultaneously, (3.8.1) may be rewritten as

$$E(E) = \bar{E} = \left[\frac{\frac{1}{m}\sum_{i=1}^{m} \bar{E}_{ij} \times \frac{1}{n}\sum_{i=1}^{n} \bar{E}_{ik} \cdots}{\frac{1}{m}\sum_{i=1}^{m} \bar{E}_{ij} + \frac{1}{n}\sum_{i=1}^{n} \bar{E}_{ik} \cdots}\right], \tag{3.8.2}$$

where $\bar{E}_{ij}$ = mean value of the ith mission effectiveness while operating in the jth mode,
$\bar{E}_{ik}$ = mean value of the ith mission effectiveness while operating in the kth mode,
m = number of missions in the jth mode,
n = number of missions in the kth mode.

Equation 3.8.2 implies that if a system is required to operate in more than one mode simultaneously the over-all effectiveness of the system will be a decreasing function (assuming mutually interfering dependence) of the number of modes required to be operated in simultaneously. In the case in which the system is to operate in more than one mode, but always in a mutually independent sequence, (3.8.2) should be replaced by

$$E(E) = \bar{E} = \frac{\frac{1}{m}\sum_{i=1}^{m} E_{ij} + \frac{1}{n}\sum_{i=1}^{n} E_{ik} \cdots}{N}, \tag{3.8.3}$$

where N = number of modes.

Both 3.8.2 and 3.8.3 will result in an unweighted average of the modes but 3.8.3 will impose no penalty on total system effectiveness simply because additional modes are added. It is conceivable, of course, that multiple-system modes, instead of being mutually interfering, could be mutually reinforcing, thereby requiring the introduction of a synergistic factor in (3.8.3).[17] In both (3.8.2) and (3.8.3) it has been assumed that all modes contribute equally to the total period effectiveness of the system.

9. TIME PHASING

Just as system costs were time phased, as shown earlier in Figure 2.7, so may system effectiveness be time phased to meet special environmental requirements. Assume that the environment within which a system will need to perform can be analyzed a priori. Assume further that this analysis reveals that the system will need to cope with a varying environment so that the intrinsic system effectiveness has to be in phase opposition to maintain a constant net effectiveness. The dynamics of

[17] The synergistic effect is discussed at greater length in Part IV.

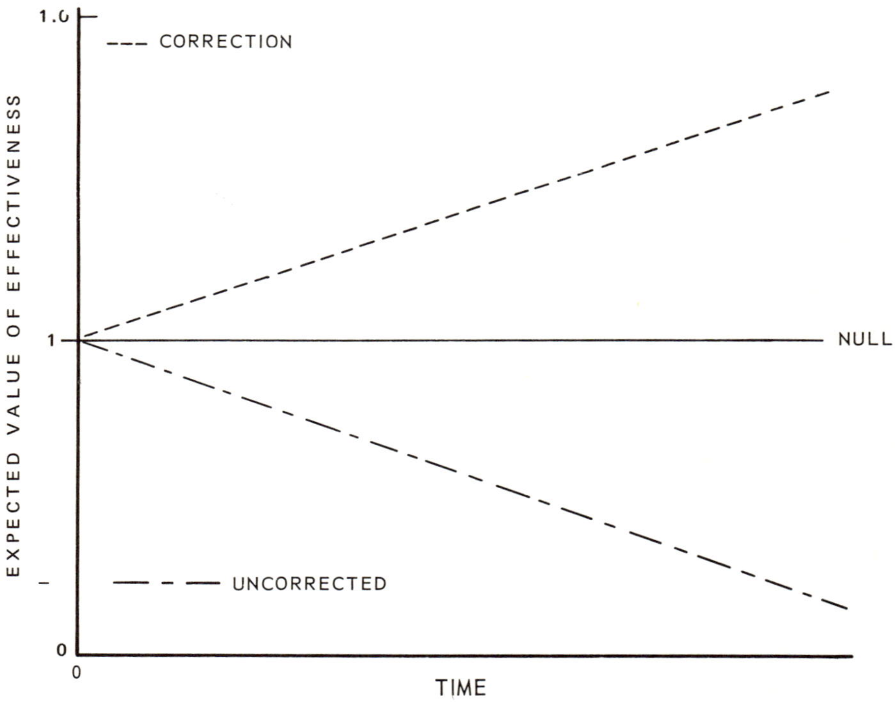

Figure 3.11

a time phased system effectiveness program may be graphically illustrated by a null diagram (see Figure 3.11).

In Figure 3.11 the system would, if uncorrected, continually decrease in effectiveness throughout the period. By incorporating a regenerative effectiveness correction of the same phase and amplitude as the degenerative force an effectiveness null may be achieved. The degenerative forces which may cause a system's effectiveness to decrease over time may be endogenous and/or exogenous in nature. Most systems will decrease in effectiveness endogenously by the insidious ravages of aging; however, the more elusive degenerative forces are exogenous and therefore usually more difficult to approximate.

In military systems analyses the exogenous degenerative forces that may affect the effectiveness of a system are those posed by the intelligence department's scenarios of projected enemy activity, which of course, has its commercial counterpart in the industrial spy's intelligence reports on projected competitor activity.

10. PROBABILISTIC EFFECTIVENESS

The development of system effectiveness in terms of a probability distribution differs from the development of the system cost-probability distribution discussed earlier in Part II. The system effectiveness expression evolved so far is based on the product or convolution of the central tendency value of the probability distribution functions of each of the independent variables involved (P, A, R, S). The resultant product $E(E)$ is therefore a single value.

To derive a probability distribution function around this resultant single value $E(E)$ would require that multiple samples $S_1 \ldots S_n$ be drawn from the respective population probability distributions of (P, A, R, S). In this manner a series of central tendency values would be obtained for each of the variables (P, A, R, S) with every sampling. The resultant series of effectiveness values $E(E_1) \ldots E(E_n)$ obtained from each of the samplings would then approximate the probability distribution function of the aggregation with its own expected value $E(E^*)$. This procedure could obviously be exceedingly artificial, even for simple systems and therefore a computer simulation model based on a Monte Carlo random sampling technique would be most useful for this kind of problem.[18]

Having developed the cost model in Part II and the effectiveness

[18] See Thomas H. Naylor, Joseph L. Balintfy, Donald S. Burdick, and Kong Chu, *Computer Simulation Techniques,* Wiley, New York, 1966.

model in Part III, it now remains to combine these models in an over-all model of system cost-effectiveness, which is the subject matter of Part IV.

SUGGESTED READINGS

- Churchman, C. West, Russel L. Ackoff, and E. Leonard Arnoff. *Introduction to Operations Research.* Wiley, New York, 1957. An excellent pedagogical text on the application of operations research to industrial and community problems.
- Croxton, Frederick E., and Dudley J. Cowden. *Applied General Statistics.* Prentice-Hall, Englewood Cliffs, N.J., 1955. An excellent general textbook on statistics recommended particularly for its treatment of statistical significance.
- Naylor, Thomas H., Joseph L. Balintfy, Donald S. Burdick, and Kong Chu. *Computer Simulation Techniques.* Wiley, New York, 1966. One of the best general books available on computer-simulation techniques.
- Morse, Philip M., and George E. Kimball. *Methods of Operations Research,* 1st ed. rev. M.I.T. Technology Press and Wiley, New York, 1951. A classic reference in operations research, especially in the field of military problems.
- Sandler, Gerald, H. *System Reliability Engineering.* Prentice-Hall, Englewood Cliffs, N.J., 1963. A comprehensive text on applied reliability.

General Notation Used in Part IV

M = cost-effectiveness figure of merit
$E(M)$ = expected value of the cost-effectiveness figure of merit
M_k = cost-effectiveness figure of merit of the ith and jth systems combined
λ = M_k/M_i = synergistic multiplier
N_i = number of units of ith system
N_j = number of units of jth system

Part IV

SYSTEM COST-EFFECTIVENESS MODELS

In this, the final part, the integration of the previously derived system cost and effectiveness models takes place. The purpose of the integration is to combine the expected values of system cost and effectiveness into a single common index for each alternative. These indices then provide the basic framework for a rational cost-effectiveness decision-making process. In seeking a rational decision-making process in this context, it must not be overlooked that any such process, although perhaps rational, will nevertheless be an imperfect procedure at best. System cost-effectiveness models are merely analytical analogs of the physical systems they represent. The resources to be expended and the effectiveness to be expected are in the final analysis only estimates based on the fundamental assumption that such models can be used to predict the future realization of systems objectives. Not only are such models intrinsically limited in their predictive capability but the system decision can rarely be based solely on the cost-effectiveness model criterion alone. The remainder of the text therefore is devoted to a description of the principles, practices, limitations, and other considerations involved in the measurement of system cost-effectiveness.

1. DOMAIN OF FEASIBILITY

First, it is suggested that before proceeding with the development of system cost-effectiveness models an evaluation be made of the cost and effectiveness inputs with respect to over-all system limitations:

> It may be that on occasion one or more of the possible alternative system configurations exceeds or is below acceptable cost and/or effectiveness thresholds. It is prudent to search for these abnormalities as early as possible, thereby minimizing the number of systems for further consideration.

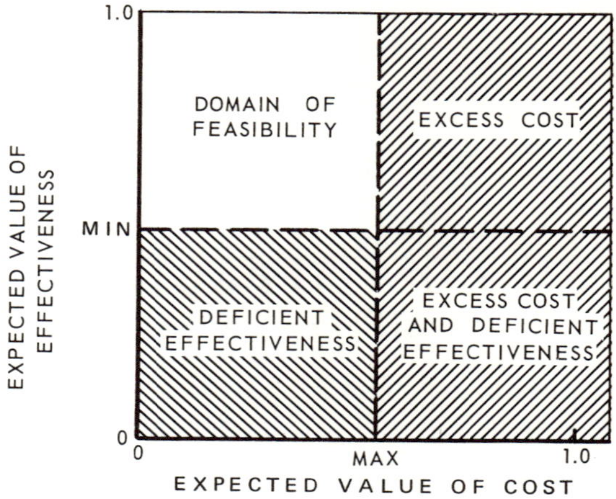

Figure 4.1

This threshold filtering process will limit the graphical field of system alternatives to a northwest corner "domain of feasibility" when the ordinate scale is effectiveness and the abscissa is cost, as shown in Figure 4.1.

If the number of remaining systems should eventually be reduced by cost and/or effectiveness limitations to a single alternative, the analysis would be without a relative comparison, in which case a rejected alternative could be used to provide a hypothetical system reference.

2. HOMOGENEITY

A second procedure preliminary to the actual development of measures of system cost-effectiveness is to examine the remaining alternatives within the domain of feasibility to be certain that they are homogeneous with respect to time, geography, possession, and scale if the most equitable and meaningful comparisons are to be made. That these desiderata of homogeneity be discussed would almost seem unnecessary, except that there are instances in which the alternatives may be heterogeneous with respect to one or more of these factors. It is felt that some discussion of each of these problem areas should be presented as a guide in meeting this requirement.

Time

Heterogeneity in time usually arises from neglecting to recognize that the systems with the longer periods to the date of obtainability should have their figure of merit penalized if equitable comparisons are to be made; for example, consider three systems with three different dates of obtainability. Assume that no system has the ideal combination of minimum cost, maximum effectiveness, and current obtainability. Decisions confronted by such dilemmas could be resolved, provided obtainability were rationally quantified. A method of penalizing cost (hence penalizing the figure of merit as a function of obtainability) was given in Part I under obtainability cost.[1]

Geography

Geographic heterogeneities may arise whenever the system alternatives are cost and/or effectiveness sensitive to geographical differences. A method of adjusting system costs to give recognition to the geographic locale was also presented in Part I. The geographic locale, however, can also have an important bearing on system effectiveness. Therefore adjustments in the effectiveness as well as the cost may need to be made in those systems that are sensitive to the geographic factor.

Possession

This type of heterogeneity arises whenever the systems being compared are in the possession of crews with different skill levels. These skill differences can significantly affect the cost of the operation as well as the effectiveness of a system. Systems displaced in time may also come into the possession of crews with different skill levels, thereby requiring an adjustment for both heterogeneities.

Scale

Homogeneities with respect to scale permit not only the identification of the systems that have the highest figure of merit but also the systems, if any, that show a net gain in savings or returns with respect to their cost. Since the costs of most systems are reckoned in monetary units, the conversion of the expected values of system effectiveness into a monetary scale translates the figure of merit, in effect, into a figure of gain; for example, the cost of a warning system may be justified in terms of the protection it affords by the avoidance of even greater costs that would be incurred without a warning system. In the final analysis it is not only necessary to identify the system that has the highest figure of merit but also whether that figure of merit provides a favorable payoff. Both objectives can be met with the ratio model described next.

[1] See also Karl Seiler, *A Cost-Effectiveness Comparison Involving a Tradeoff of Performance, Cost and Obtainability*, *J. ORSA*, **14**, 528–531, 1966.

3. RATIO MODEL

The ratio cost-effectiveness model basically measures the "efficiency" of a system in terms of the ratio of its output (effectiveness) to its input (cost). As such, it is merely the division of the system effectiveness index by the system cost index which results in an over-all figure of merit as the quotient. This simple relationship offers the most expeditious means of comparing alternative systems. The procedure may be further simplified by normalizing the system cost indices, so that together with the already normalized system effectiveness indices a normalized figure of merit can be obtained. The notational definition is

$$E(M_i) = \frac{E(E_i)}{E(C_i)} \leqq 1.0, \tag{4.3.1}$$

where $E(M_i) = \bar{M}_i$ = expected value of the cost-effectiveness figure of merit of the ith system,

$E(E_i) = \bar{E}_i$ = expected value of the effectiveness of the ith system,

$E(C_i) = \bar{C}_i$ = expected value of the total cost of the ith system.

Figures of merit may then be calculated by using (4.3.1) for any set of alternatives in which either the system cost or the system effectiveness is held constant, as shown in Figure 4.2*a* and *b*, respectively. Of the three alternatives shown for each of the constant cost and constant effectiveness cases, the preferred alternative is circled, since it represents the highest effectiveness obtainable for a given cost or, conversely, the least-cost solution for a given effectiveness. It frequently happens, how-

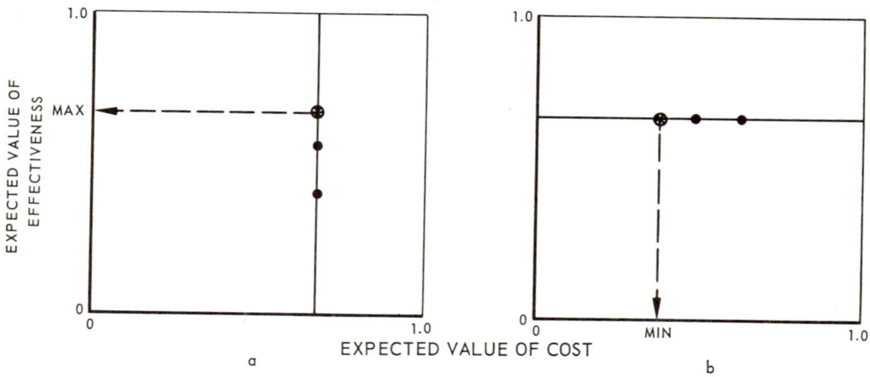

Figure 4.2

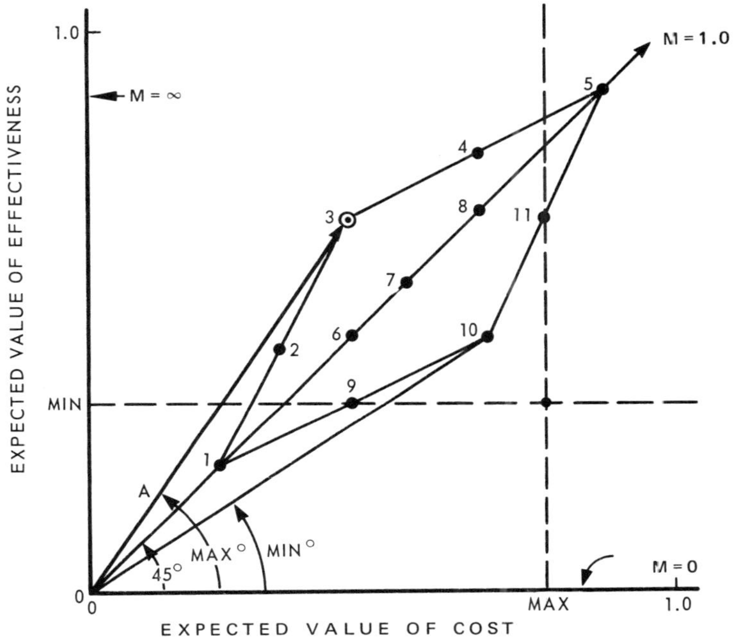

Figure 4.3

ever, that the alternative systems do not afford a constant cost or a constant effectiveness comparison, as shown in Figure 4.2, because both the cost and the effectiveness are variables. To illustrate the ambiguity involved consider a plot of numerous alternatives, as shown in Figure 4.3.

Note that the cloud of alternatives tapered about the 45° axis represents a diminution of alternatives at the extreme cost-effectiveness intersection areas. This is merely a manifestation of the problem that it becomes increasingly more difficult to configure systems with lower and lower cost and, conversely, increasingly more difficult to stretch the state of the art in system effectiveness. The following observations are made concerning Figure 4.3:

1. Systems 1 and 5 are clearly infeasible because of deficient effectiveness and excess cost.
2. Systems 9 and 11 are borderline feasibility systems.
3. System 3 lies on that vector **A** from the origin which has the greatest slope hence represents the highest figure of merit attainable.

4. System 2 is the next best figure of merit system because it represents the point through which the next highest slope vector would pass and so on through the entire group down to system 10 which has the lowest figure of merit of the group; systems 1, 5, 6, 7, and 8 are ambiguous re E(M).

5. System 4 affords the greatest effectiveness within the feasible region.

6. System 6 is irrelevant because for the same cost system 3 provides greater effectiveness and is said to dominate system 6. Similarly, system 8 is irrelevant, since it is dominated by system 4.

In summary, the procedure to locate the alternative with the highest figure of merit in any distribution of alternatives on a planar cost-effectiveness graph is as follows:

1. Establish the domain of feasibility by erecting the maximum cost limit ordinate and the minimum effectiveness limit abscissa coordinates.[2]
2. Sweep a vector from the origin through the point that represents the maximum angular sweep possible through any of the points.
3. Determine the coordinate values of the point lying on the highest angular vector and compute the figure of merit by using (4.3.1).

Optimal Efficiency System versus Optimal Effectiveness System

In Part I, it was stated that the output of an activity should, if possible, be expanded only as long as the marginal benefit exceeds the marginal cost (see Figure 1.5). The same reasoning applies in Figure 4.3, so that although system 3 has the highest figure of merit and is therefore the optimal efficiency alternative system 4 is the optimal effectiveness choice within the limit of resources allowed.

Limitations

Although the ratio cost-effectiveness model is based on a relatively simple concept, it is also limited in the interpretations that can be made from it. Its chief limitation arises from the fact that a ratio may be used to express an output whose return is optimal versus an output, the efficiency of which is optimal (see Figure 1.5). This disadvantage, however, is not an intrinsic weakness in the mathematical procedure but merely reflects the necessity of identifying the quotient values in terms of their coordinate determinants. Another limitation of the ratio model is its inability to handle combinations of alternatives, since it does not contain any information concerning the functional relationship between alternatives; for example, given three system alternatives (A,

[2] In the example given this is the northwest or (II) quadrant. Reversing the scales, however, shifts the feasibility domain to the southeast or (IV) quadrant.

B, and C), a ratio model may disclose that A is preferred to B and B is preferred to C; $A > B > C$. However, the ratio model is incapable of revealing whether A and B in some combination might indeed be better than A alone; $A + B > A$. This leads logically to the next subject of indifference curve models which are capable of resolving whether some combination of systems is preferable to any discrete system acting alone.

4. INDIFFERENCE CURVE MODEL

The indifference curve[3] model is, of course, a more complex device than the ratio model described previously. Many systems therefore never reach this level of analysis because of the scarcity of time, funds, and interested personnel. The result is that the indifference curve model is used rather infrequently in cost-effectiveness analyses, notwithstanding its superiority. The description of an indifference curve model for analyzing the effectiveness of various combinations of two systems is given first, followed by a description of means to handle three and greater than three combinations of systems.

Combinations of Two Systems

Consider two physically differentiated systems, i and j, each of which is normally procured in multiple identical units. Assume for simplicity that the expected value of total system cost for each unit of either system is the same:

$$E(C_i) = E(C_j). \tag{4.4.1}$$

Assume further that the expected value of unit effectiveness of either system is the same:

$$E(E_i) = E(E_j). \tag{4.4.2}$$

By combining (4.4.1) and (4.4.2) the figure of merit of system i is equated with that of system j:

$$E(M_i) = E(M_j) = \frac{E(E_i)}{E(C_i)} = \frac{E(E_j)}{E(C_j)}. \tag{4.4.3}$$

The decision maker could, under these circumstances, choose either all units of system i, all units of system j, or any combination thereof, since the cost would be the same and the figure of merit would be unchanged as shown in Figure 4.4.[4]

[3] Indifference curves are also referred to as isoquant curves.

[4] A further assumption implied here is that of nonsatiety, meaning that the decision maker is not oversupplied with either system and therefore prefers more of i and/or j.

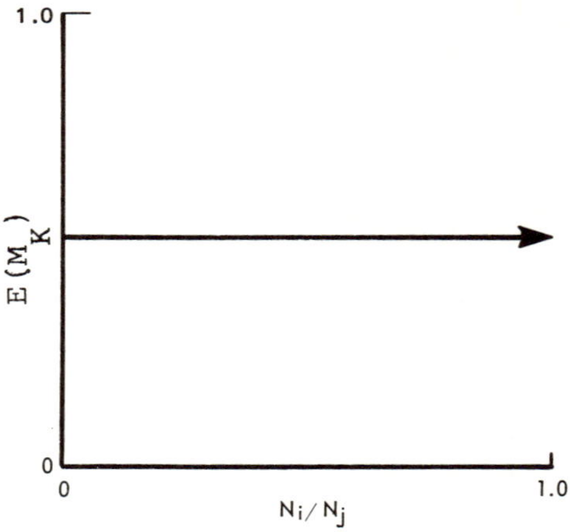

Figure 4.4

Figure 4.4 implies a constant marginal rate of substitution between systems *i* and *j*. This means that the decision maker is always willing to give up the same number of units of system *i* for system *j* and vice versa, regardless of his holdings of either *i* or *j*. This may also be seen in Figure 4.5 in terms of a linear indifference curve *I*, where the exchanges at points *a* and *b* are the same and indeed would be the same

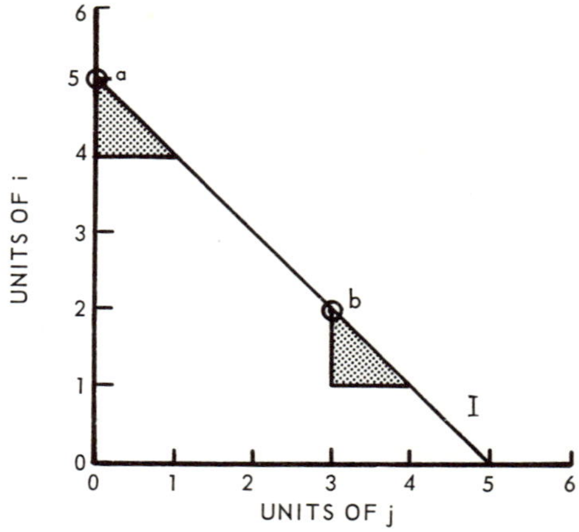

Figure 4.5

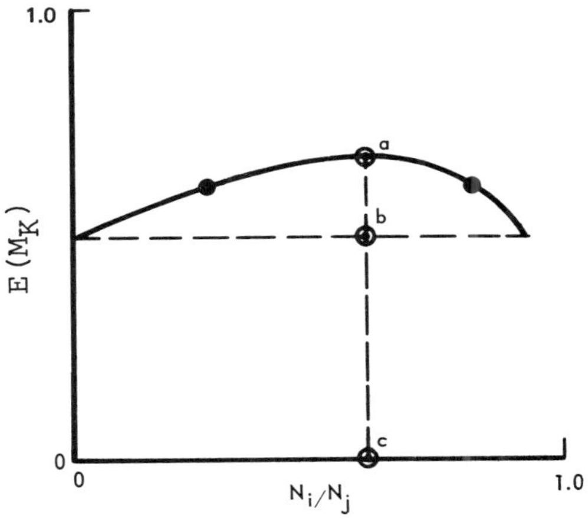

Figure 4.6

along any linear indifference curve.[5] If it is known that the marginal rate of substitution between two alternatives is a constant, free interchange between the alternatives is permissible and all combinations would have the same figure of merit shown in Figure 4.4.

If, however, the marginal rate of substitution between the alternatives is either unknown or known to be variable, free interchange between the alternatives may no longer be feasible and certain combinations of systems may exhibit a higher figure of merit than others, as shown in Figure 4.6. Line *ac* in Figure 4.6, when divided by line *bc*, defines a multiplier λ which is a measure of the maximum increase in the figure of merit obtainable over that obtained when using all of either alternative separately[6]:

$$E(M_k) = \lambda E(M_i) = \lambda E(M_j). \tag{4.4.4}$$

Point *c*, in Figure 4.6, defines the optimum combination of alternatives which, of course, is determined by finding that combination of alternatives which maximizes the figure of merit. This is readily done by incor-

[5] An indifference curve may be defined as a locus of points of equal satisfaction; hence an indifference exists as to where along such a curve one may choose to allocate alternatives, since all allocations by definition produce the same degree of satisfaction. As long as the decision maker is not oversupplied with either alternative, the indifference curve will have a negative slope.

[6] Line *ab* is a measure of the synergism of the combination of systems. Of course, combinations of certain systems may be incompatible (antienergistic), in which case the curve in Figure 4.6 would be inverted and λ would be less than unity.

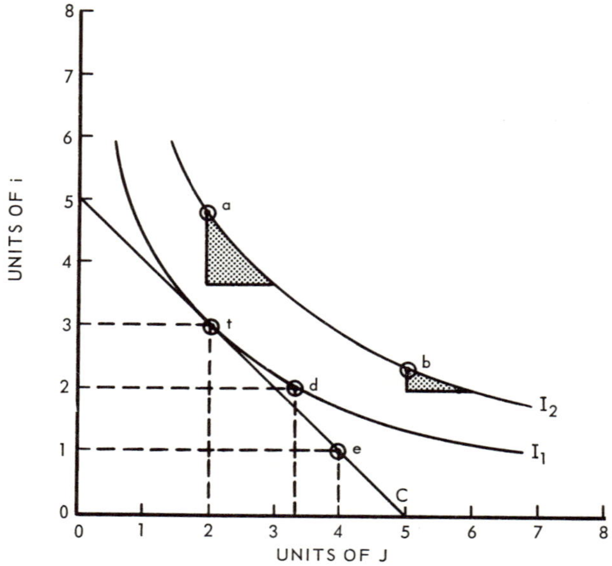

Figure 4.7

porating into Figure 4.5 a constant cost curve C along with a series of *nonlinear* indifference curves I_1 and I_2, as shown in Figure 4.7.

In Figure 4.7 the indifference curves I_1 and I_2 represent a diminishing marginal rate of substitution of system i for system j. At point a the decision maker is willing to give up a larger number of units of system i for an additional unit of system j than he is willing to give up at point b, where i is in relative scarcity. The absolute slope of the indifference curve therefore diminishes toward the right and presents a convex profile to the origin. The indifference curve I_2 is simply a locus of satisfaction higher than that of I_1 and for the purpose of this discussion represents a higher level of system effectiveness than that of I_1. The indifference curve that lies above and to the right of another always represents a preferred combination of alternatives. Furthermore, the indifference curves can never meet or intersect if the decision maker is not satiated with either alternative and is transitive[7] with respect to all combinations of alternatives. The constant cost curve C represents

[7] If x, y, and z are any three combinations of alternative systems along an indifference curve and if x is indifferent with respect to y and y is indifferent with respect to z, the decision maker is transitive if he is indifferent between x and z.

a fixed budget with which the decision maker can procure all units of i, all units of j, or any combination thereof.

The interpretation of the curves in Figure 4.7 from a cost-effectiveness viewpoint is as follows:

1. The cost curve C describes the manner in which the alternative systems can be exchanged in terms of procurement for a given constant budget.

2. The indifference curves I_1 and I_2 describe the manner in which the alternative systems can be exchanged while maintaining the effectiveness constant.

3. At any point of tangency t any further exchange of one alternative for the other cannot increase the effectiveness.

4. The only manner in which to achieve the effectiveness level of I_2 is to secure a higher budget.

5. Any other point such as d would be nonoptimum, since it requires a higher budget (2 units of i and 3.4 units of j, assuming that the system units can be effectively divided).

6. The optimum system combination is therefore three units of i and two units of j, since it is the only combination that can result in the attainment of an effectiveness level of I_1. Similarly, the procurement

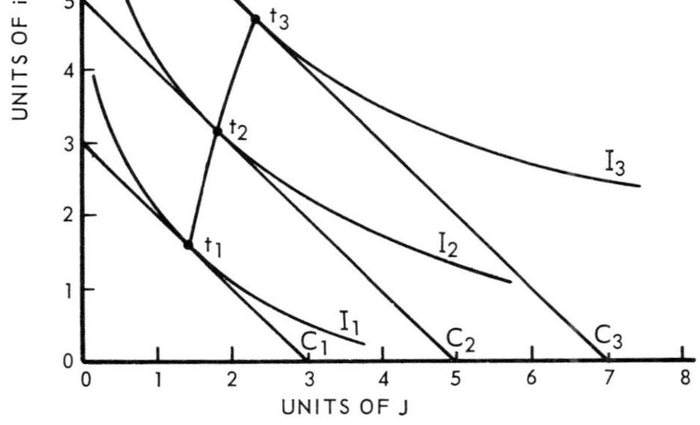

Figure 4.8

of one unit of i and four units of j at the given budget would clearly result in attaining significantly less than an effectiveness level of I_1.

Indifference curve analyses may be made similarly for various budget levels such as C_1, C_2, and C_3, as shown in Figure 4.8. Connecting the points of tangency t_1, t_2, and t_3 in Figure 4.8 defines an isocline. The isocline in turn defines an income consumption curve when $C_1 \ldots C_3$ are consumer[8] budgets by which the variations in the consumer's purchases of systems i and j as his income changes are described. When $C_1 \ldots C_3$ are production budgets, the isocline describes the expansion path of the change in a firm's optimum combination of inputs i and j as the firm's budget for inputs increases.

Combinations of Three and > Three Systems

When there are three system alternatives from which to choose, the cost and indifference curves would become three-dimensional surfaces

[8] The consumer is broadly defined to include the decision maker faced with a number of alternative systems for procurement.

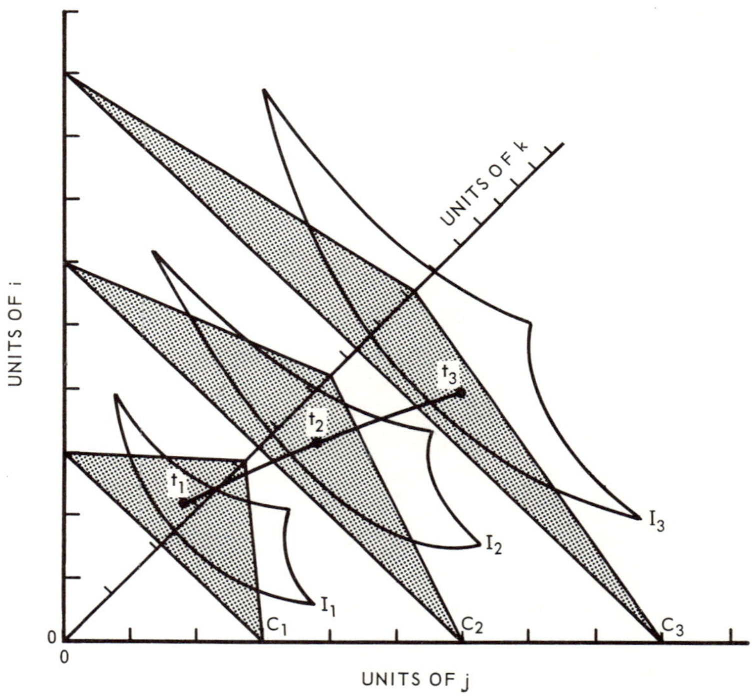

Figure 4.9

as shown in Figure 4.9. The points of tangency t_1, t_2, and t_3 in Figure 4.8 then become points of contact between the surfaces shown in Figure 4.9. The three coordinate values for each of the contact points then uniquely define the optimum combination of the three alternatives at each stage. When there are greater than three alternative systems, the cost and indifference curves merely become n dimensional surfaces.

Limitations

Although the indifference curve cost-effectiveness models just described are more useful than the simple ratio model described earlier, they too have their limitations:

1. Whenever system specifications may be stated as precise values, these models can usually be used to identify the optimum combination of systems by the use of ordinary calculus techniques. This is true, however, only if the graphs of the equations of the specifications (the mathematician's side conditions) are not kinked or discontinuous. Since the calculus method depends on a slope analysis, kinks or discontinuities preclude slope definition and will rule out these models.
2. System specifications may not be precise and state only the minimum requirements, in which case the side conditions are inequalities instead of equations. The presence of inequalities may again rule out the calculus approach, since the minimum requirement specification may mask the true optimum combination of systems which might be somewhere below the minimum requirement and therefore never be discovered.

Fortunately, these limitations can be largely overcome by the use of the so-called programming methods described next.

5. MATHEMATICAL PROGRAMMING

Mathematical programming is a vast subject that embraces linear, nonlinear, integer, and dynamic programming, the calculus of variations, and optimal control theory. Linear programming assumes that all the variations within a system's variables are linear, whereas nonlinear programming permits this assumption to be relaxed. Integer programming permits the variations within a system's variables to be discontinuous functions of discrete values. Dynamic programming, the calculus of variations, and optimal control theory are all concerned with the optimality of processes over time.

It would serve no useful purpose to review all of this material in order to demonstrate its potential in the analysis of cost-effectiveness problems. Instead a heuristic approach is felt to be the best alternative, since the subject matter is exceptionally well covered in the material of the several specialists referenced at the end of Part IV. Accordingly, all that will be attempted is a demonstration of the similarity of a linear programming problem and the indifference curve-price line model already described. In fact, the linear programming model embodies the same indifference-curve isoquant concept developed in the preceding section.

Linear programming, first used in the solution of military problems toward the close of World War II, has expanded tremendously in the intervening years. Typical linear programming problems today range from determining the optimum allocation of a firm's productive resources among the competing products for those resources to deriving minimum cost transportation networks. Costly experimentation and sheer guessing are essentially eliminated by the use of linear programming in particular and mathematical programming in general.

The application of linear programming to cost-effectiveness problems is, of course, not new.[9] The fundamental nature of the technique of linear programming is best described in terms of a simple graphical illustration. Consider an automotive plant in which the investment in capital equipment permits the production of only two major automotive product lines—passenger cars and light trucks. The graph of such a problem may be simply a two-dimensional field in which the respective product-line outputs are dimensioned on the ordinate and abscissa scales, as shown in Figure 4.10. As already noted, linear programming problems are uniquely characterized by the presence of side conditions, which may be equations of specifications whose graphs are kinked or discontinuous or inequalities rather than equations. In Figure 4.10 the side conditions are inequalities represented by the lines BB' (body capacity limitation) and EE' (engine capacity limitation). Any point on BB' will satisfy the inequality, hence use all of the body-producing capacity; also, any point to the left and below BB' will also satisfy the inequality but at less than full capacity. The output of cars and trucks must also satisfy the engine inequality EE' which may be satisfied, like BB', either completely or partly. Since there are two inequalities, the satisfaction of both can be only to the left and below both BB' and EE', thereby defining a feasibility boundary BCE'. By imposing two additional inequalities (that the outputs of both product lines must be ≥ 0) a feasibility region $ABCE'$ is defined. In essence the feasibility region defines all those output combinations that are within the plant's capacity.

[9] See Bernard S. Albert, *Cost-Effectiveness Evaluation for Mixes of Naval Air Weapons Systems, J. ORSA,* **11,** 173–193, 1963, which describes the use of linear programming in the weapon-system selection process.

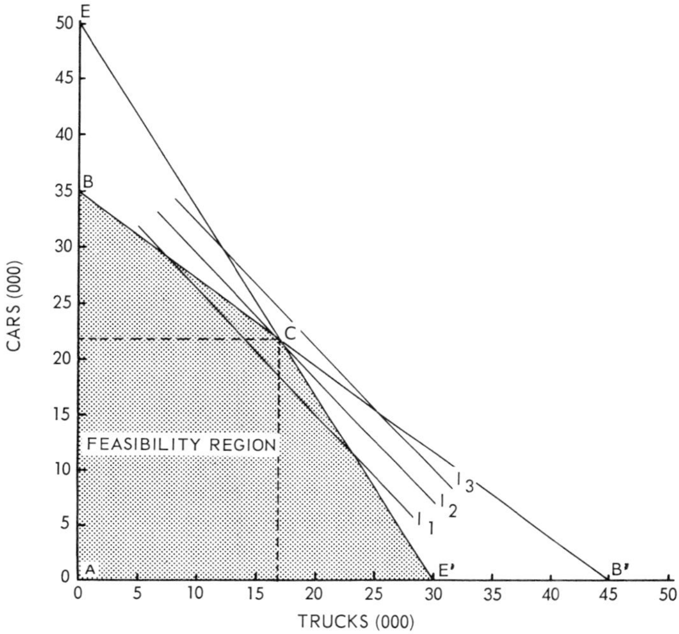

Figure 4.10

By introducing an objective function (in this example it is assumed that the management is attempting to maximize profits) the quantity of outputs which optimizes the objective function may be identified. In Figure 4.10 the objective function is represented by the three linear profit indifference curves, I_1, I_2, and I_3. Since this is a linear program, the profit indifference curves are straight lines and they will not intersect or meet for the same reasons given in Section 4.[10] The optimal output of cars and trucks in Figure 4.10 is represented by point C, which is unique in that it is the only point on the feasibility boundary whose coordinate values will produce the highest profit attainable, represented by I_2. The coordinate values producing the highest profit are 22,000 cars and 17,000 trucks, and any other output combination would therefore be nonoptimal.

The example just given of an automotive plant linear programming problem was, of course, grossly oversimplified in order to illustrate the principle involved. When the number of side conditions increases, the

[10] See p. 80.

number of segments in the feasibility boundary will increase, thereby producing more corners. In general the procedure in any linear programming problem is to search along the feasibility boundary for the corner that is optimal.[11] This procedure, of course, may be accomplished graphically for the smaller problems, but it is best done on a computer for the larger problems. Geometrically, the similarity between a linear programming problem and the indifference curve-price line problem described in Section 4 is clear. The graph of the indifference curve-price line model is an example of the convolution of a convex (to the origin) indifference curve with a linear price line. The graph of the linear programming model is an example of the convolution of a concave (to the origin) polyhedron with a linear indifference curve.

The discussions of the ratio model, the indifference curve model, and the various mathematical programming models have all implicitly assumed a decision maker operating in a vacuum with respect to all other decision makers in his field. This idyllic assumption, however, can never be made in any competitive system, be it military or commercial. The decision maker must weigh all the possible reactions to his various possible decisions if he is to choose the best possible strategy against all opponent strategies. This is the essence of the theory of games and is therefore discussed next.

6. THEORY OF GAMES

The theory of games is devoted to the identification of optimal strategies in conflict confrontations. The objective in this section is to show the relationship between a gaming problem and a cost-effectiveness problem. This is done in two ways: first by deduction and second by example.

It was shown in Section 5 on mathematical programming that there was indeed, in linear programming, a striking similarity to the so-called indifference curve model. The linear programming model is essentially a specialized form of the indifference curve model, used whenever the variables are constrained by side conditions.

That there is a strong relationship between game theory and linear programming was first pointed out by J. von Neumann in 1947 in discussions with George B. Dantzig.[12] In those discussions von Neumann "showed that the central mathematical problem associated with a matrix

[11] In the case in which the indifference curve may be parallel to a segment of the feasibility boundary the whole segment including its corners may become optimal.

[12] See George B. Dantzig, *Linear Programming and Extensions,* Princeton University Press, Princeton, N.J., 1963, p. 277.

game could be stated as a linear program and he conjectured that the converse was true."[13] By way of the logic of association, therefore, game theory is related to the solution of the indifference curve cost-effectiveness problem. That this is indeed the case may be demonstrated with a simple example, since any attempt to cover game theory completely is neither intended nor necessary. Again the heuristic approach is felt to be by far the best alternative.

The game to be presented is a zero sum, two-person game with a min-max solution.[14] The term zero sum simply means that the gain of the one player always equals the loss of the other player. It is shown in the example that the equilibrium strategy for both players results in neither player obtaining his nonequilibrium maximum return. Consider the following competitive example: there are two contenders, x and y, vying militarily or commercially for a market or territory. There are three basic approaches that x and y might take, based on their past performances and level of sophistication in strategic planning:

1. If neither x nor y knows anything of game theory and of each other's counterstrategies, the contest would be reduced to a pure guessing game.
2. If either x or y could predict the other's counterstrategies based on past observations or espionage, either x or y could choose an optimal strategy, a priori, without resorting to game theory.
3. If neither x nor y can predict the other's counterstrategies, but both used the theory of games, it would be possible for x and y to choose their best strategies without any specific counterstrategy knowledge.

The only required information for using the theory of games is the payoffs that will accrue to x and y over the range of strategies available to them, assumed for simplicity to be only three for each. These payoffs represent the effectiveness levels attainable by x and y and, again for simplicity, are assumed to be the result of the same expenditure by each. The payoffs for x are conveniently described in a matrix format as shown in Figure 4.11. The payoff matrix for y is simply the complement of x's payoff matrix ($100 - x$'s share $= y$'s share). The y entries in the matrix represent y's choice of counterstrategy to x's strategies. Similarly, the x entries in the matrix represent x's choice of counterstrategy to y's strategies.

[13] *Ibid.*

[14] See John von Neumann and Oskar Morgenstern, *Theory of Games and Economic Behavior,* 3rd ed., Princeton University Press, Princeton, N.J., 1953.

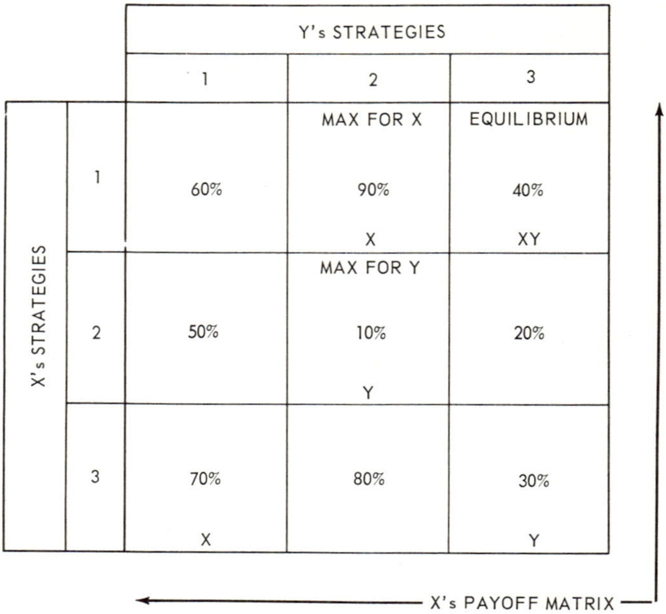

Figure 4.11

The analysis of the respective strategies of x and y in Figure 4.11 reveals that the best strategy for x and the best strategy for y results in the establishment of an equilibrium. The best strategy for x is No. 1, the maximin (see entries in Table 4.1), which yields x a 40 percent

Table 4.1

If x Uses Strategy	y Uses Counter-strategy	Effectiveness Yield in Percent for x	y
No. 1	No. 3	40 max	60 min
No. 2	No. 2	10	90
No. 3	No. 3	30	70

effectiveness level. The best strategy for y is No. 3, the minimax (see entries in Table 4.2), which yields y a 60 percent effectiveness level.

An equilibrium occurs when x uses strategy No. 1 and y uses strategy No. 3; the result is that x receives 40 percent effectiveness and y receives

60 percent effectiveness. The equilibrium is y's best counterstrategy to x's best strategy and vice versa. That this equilibrium is the maximum for neither x nor y may be seen by referring again to Figure 4.11. The absolute maximum for x is seen to be 90 percent effectiveness if x were to choose strategy No. 1 and y were to choose strategy No. 2; likewise the absolute maximum for y is seen to be 90 percent effectiveness if y were to choose strategy No. 2 and x were to choose strategy No. 2.

Table 4.2

If y Uses Strategy	x Uses Counter-strategy	Effectiveness Yield in Percent for x	Effectiveness Yield in Percent for y
No. 1	No. 3	70	30
No. 2	No. 1	90	10
No. 3	No. 1	40 min	60 max

The reader should be aware that the results of a game theory strategy may not always end in an equilibrium, as may be seen in the simple 2×2 matrix game in Figure 4.12, in which x's best strategy, No. 2, yields x 50 percent effectiveness and y's best strategy, No. 1, yields y 30 percent effectiveness. As a result there is no coincidence of strategies, hence no equilibrium, and an unstable game is created. It should also

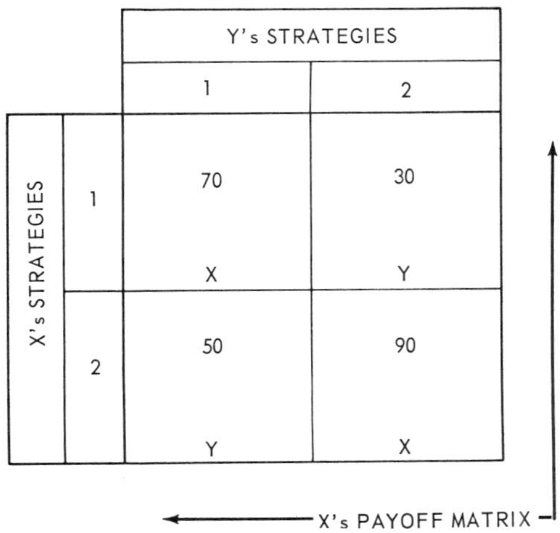

Figure 4.12

be mentioned that the choice of a game theory strategy will be optimal only against an opponent who is also using game theory strategy. Referring again to Figure 4.11, if y chooses strategy No. 1, x's best strategy is No. 3, which yields x 70 percent effectiveness, as compared with x's maximin strategy No. 1 which yields x only 40 percent effectiveness in equilibrium with y.

That the application of game theory to real-world problems is as simple as the examples given might suggest is not the case in many instances. In practice there are frequently complicating and limiting factors present, some or all of which may be involved:

1. The reliability of the payoff matrix data may be questionable, especially in extremely dynamic situations.
2. There may be considerably more than two persons in a game.
3. The game may be of a nonconstant sum variety.
4. The game may involve mixed strategies on the part of some or all of the players.

Taking each of these factors in turn, first, the determination of even relatively simple game theory payoff matrices can be a challenging forecasting problem. The lack of control over the exogenous variables in a payoff forecast can seriously limit the statistical confidence level, if any, that can be attributed to such estimates. Second, most industries contain more than two firms and most military problems concern more than two nations. Therefore the payoff matrices are more likely to be n-dimensional, coalitions among the players may very well develop, and the whole exercise may likely rest on the outer fringe of game theory. Third, many games are really nonconstant sum in that the strategies of the various players can have a significant effect on the size of the combined payoff. This, of course, requires that additional estimates be made of the variation in the combined payoff as a function of the respective player strategies. Finally, even if a game can be reduced to the two person, zero-sum variety, your competition may quite possibly use a mixed strategy to preclude you from being able to predict his strategy.[15] A simple method of doing this merely involves picking two reasonably good strategies and then choosing from among them by means of a random selector. In essence, a mixed strategy permits greater gains as well as greater losses, the gains hopefully exceeding the losses.

By way of this brief discussion of game theory problems it is hoped that the reader will have gained some insight into the philosophy of strategic planning. It is clear that in a competitive environment a system

[15] The strategies described in the preceding examples were all so-called pure strategies with no elements of probability of occurrence.

decision based on a cost-effectiveness analysis should consider the various possible effects of competitive counterstrategies. In conclusion it cannot be denied that a game theory analysis may become a difficult undertaking, but the consequences of its neglect might be even more strenuous to bear.

7. PROBABILISTIC COST-EFFECTIVENESS

The discussion of mixed strategies in Section 6 on game theory provides a suitable transition to probabilistic cost-effectiveness, since a mixed strategy involves a purely random choice of a particular strategy from among a set of alternative strategies. A nondescript distribution of strategies is therefore presented to one's opposition as a means of preventing him from eventually identifying a pure strategy. In contrast to the use of probability theory to confuse the "enemy," its use in a cost-effectiveness analysis is to enlighten the decision maker. Just how this may be achieved is the purpose of this section. The discussion of the application of probabilistic measures of cost-effectiveness will be limited to the ratio and indifference curve models already described. Extensions to the programming and gaming models should then become obvious.

All of the system cost-effectiveness models described so far have assumed single expected values for both the cost as well as the effectiveness, thereby resulting in determinant figures of merit when using ratio models or determinant mixes of alternatives when using indifference curve models.[16] In the limit neither cost or effectiveness is determinable; therefore by recognizing that cost and effectiveness can, at best, be described only by their respective probability distributions the decision maker is enabled to weigh his confidence[17] in the various alternative systems. Considered first is the application of probability distributions of cost and effectiveness in the ratio model shown in Figure 4.13.

In Figure 4.13 three alternative systems (1, 2, and 3) are shown plotted at their most likely coordinate values as well as with their circumscribed probability limit contours. System 1 is typical of an early prototype system, the central tendency value of the figure of merit showing a high cost related to a low effectiveness, circumscribed at the two-sigma level by a rather large circle.[18] System 2, more typical of the production

[16] With the exception of the use of a mixed strategy in the theory of games, which, of course, would result in a probability distribution of the effectiveness and resultant figure of merit.

[17] Or, conversely, the degree of risk involved.

[18] Where sigma is the statistical standard error of the data and at the two-sigma level, 95 percent of the cases will be included at some chosen confidence level (see Part III, pp. 46 to 48).

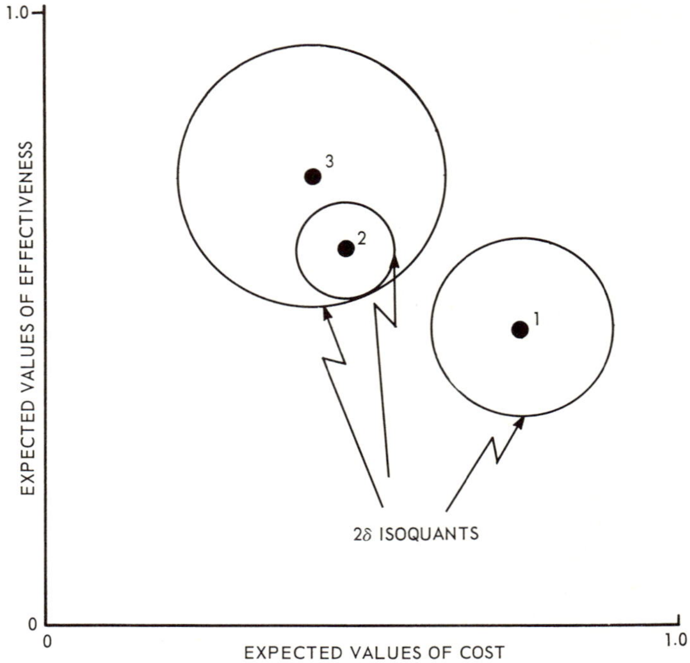

Figure 4.13

design phase of System 1, shows increased effectiveness, lowered cost, and significantly less area in the two-sigma circle. System 3 would represent the effect of a breakthrough in the state of the art, and would achieve both higher effectiveness and lower cost but with considerable uncertainty, as shown by the very large area in the two-sigma circle.

If the only concern to the decision maker was the central tendency values of the figures of merit for the three alternatives, system 3 would clearly outclass the other two systems because of its highest effectiveness and lowest cost. When the three alternatives are examined, however, in terms of the probability distributions around the central tendency value of the figures of merit, the choice is no longer clear-cut. System 3 represents to the decision maker a tradeoff choice: expectations of higher effectiveness and lower cost versus greater uncertainties in both effectiveness and cost. The probability contour for system 3 was purposely drawn to encompass the probability contour of system 2, merely to emphasize the uncertainty of system 3, it being possible for system

3 actually to cost more than system 2 and to have a lower effectiveness than system 2.

The advantage to the decision maker of alternative choices presented in terms of the confidence in their expectations is clear, decisions made otherwise will simply result in a greater percentage of decision errors. A system like 3 would always be chosen (in a no-probability context) over systems 1 and 2; however, such a choice could be wrong, as shown by the probability distributions around the central tendency values. The cost of being wrong in the cost sense may be readily determined by comparing the system's accrued actual cost versus the previous estimated cost. The cost of being wrong in the effectiveness sense, however, may never be known for some systems (e.g., an ICBM system). Wherever possible the actual effectiveness obtained should be measured and compared with the previous estimate. By combining the error in the cost with the error in the effectiveness an over-all cost-effectiveness appraisal can be made. The limits of such error combinations may extend anywhere from a dismal failure to a resounding success. A general classification of the possible variations about the expected values of system cost and system effectiveness may be made (see Table 4.3).

Table 4.3

Effectiveness	Cost	
Low	High	(worst case)
Low	Par	
Low	Low	
Par	High	
Par	Par	(no errors)
Par	Low	
High	High	
High	Par	
High	Low	(best case)

In the application of probability distributions of cost and effectiveness to the two-dimensional indifference curve type of cost-effectiveness model multiple points of tangency would be created, as shown in Figure 4.14, the probabilistic counterpart of Figure 4.8 described earlier. The two sigma limits for both effectiveness and cost uniquely define the two sigma limits for the optimal range of alternative mixes for each of the three budget levels (C_1, C_2, and C_3). The locus of the central tangential points defines an isocline as already described; however, the loci on

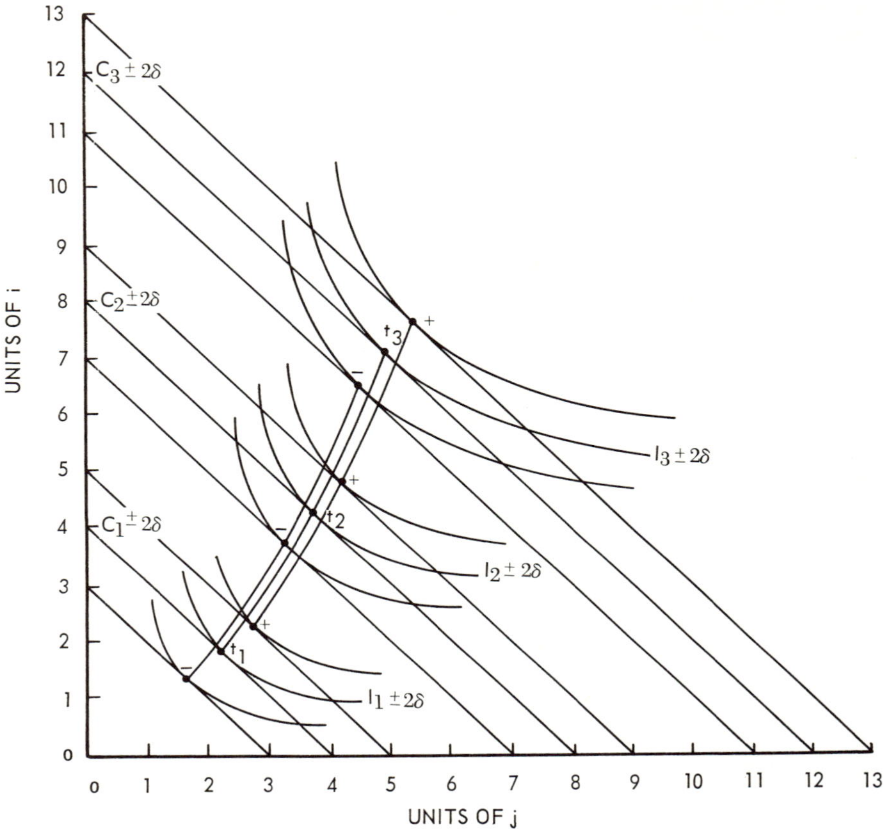

Figure 4.14

each side of the central locus now define the probabilistic limits associated with the isocline path.

When applying probability distributions of cost and effectiveness to the three-dimensional indifference curve type of cost-effectiveness model, the points of contact representing the optimal solutions, as shown earlier in Figure 4.9, become areas of contact (see Figure 4.15). The two sigma limit contours in this case define the probabilistic area limits within which an optimal mix of alternatives may fall. The isocline paths in Figure 4.15 in effect define a tube formed by the dispersion in the points of tangency between the respective surfaces.

Admittedly, the application of probability distributions in a system cost-effectiveness analysis significantly complicates the effort, even when working with relatively simple ratio models. The complication, however, is not so much the result of methodological difficulties as it is the result of a frequent lack of information on which to form any probability distributions. What is needed is a good statistical data base that contains the projected trends in the errors of the estimates of both cost and engineering functions. Unfortunately, many organizations just do not keep such records, but perhaps with the continued growth in the capabilities of machine data processing the maintenance of such statistical bases will become not only more economical but also less burdensome. When working with probabilistic indifference curve cost-effectiveness models, even more information is required to derive probabilistic marginal rates of substitution. It is at this point in current cost-effectiveness practice that the very frontier of the discipline looms into view. Figures 4.14 and 4.15 are therefore not representative of contemporary applied cost-effectiveness practices but are rather more conceptually idealistic and theoretical in nature. The reduction of these idealized concepts even to a limited pragmatic practice will probably require not only considerable enlargement of the existing data bases in many organizations but also a considerable development in the technique of effectively measuring

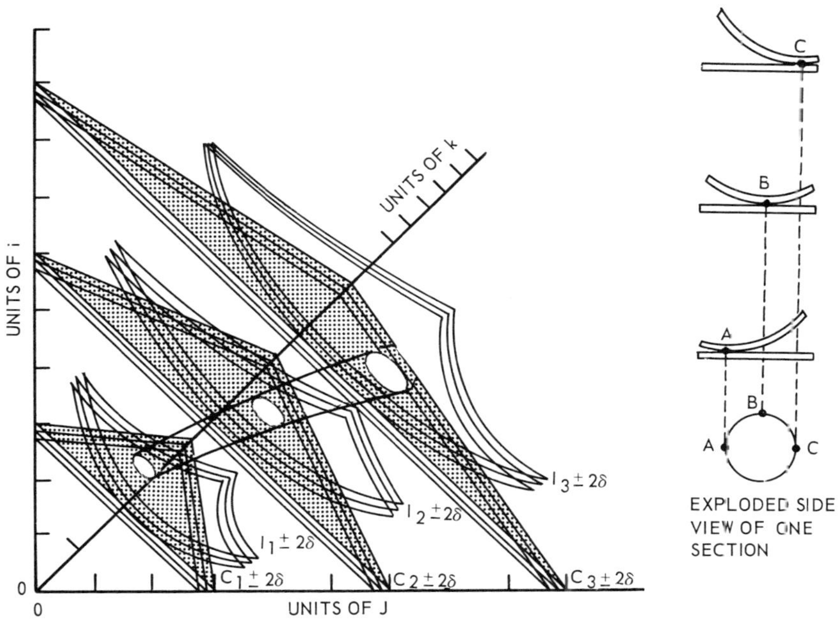

Figure 4.15

marginal rates of substitution. In summary, since the development of probabilistic indifference curve system cost-effectiveness models is currently not far advanced, the next best immediate alternative is at least to attempt to measure the probabilities associated with the measurement of effectiveness and cost in ratio. Whenever possible, the need for probabilistic cost-effectiveness measures should be anticipated to permit the timely preparation of whatever additional statistical data base may be necessary, beforehand. In this regard it is also well to anticipate early in a system cost-effectiveness study the need for considering those broad exogenous factors that could have an effect on the choice among the various possible alternatives. A discussion of some of the more prevalent types of exogenous influence that could have a bearing on the outcome of a system cost-effectiveness decision is reserved for the next and last section in this part.

8. DECISION MAKING AND THE COST-EFFECTIVENESS CRITERION

The application of any of the various methodologies described in the foregoing pages can provide only at best a numerical figure of merit series on which to base a decision. It should be clearly understood, however, that any such decision in a systems context usually cannot be realistically made solely on the basis of the endogenous considerations of cost and effectiveness alone. The various exogenous factors that may impinge on the result of a system decision based solely on the criteria of cost and effectiveness can be overwhelming and therefore cannot be casually disregarded. Unfortunately, however, these exogenous factors are usually not amenable to an objective analysis because of their highly unpredictable nature. The decision maker, therefore, intent on choosing an alternative with the choicest figure of merit, must re-examine the efficacy of that choice in the light of these exogenous factors. The chief factors in this category that may have a significant influence on system choice are as follows:

1. Technological advances
2. Resource availability
3. Political sensitivity
4. Psychological stimulus

A useful aid in resolving problems of this nature, in which there is a multitude of system alternatives and criteria and the decisions pertaining thereto are sequential, is to use a stochastic decision tree.[19] A decision

[19] Russell D. Archibald and Richard L. Villoria, *Network-Based Management Systems (PERT/CPM)*, Wiley, New York, 1967.

tree based on network theory consists of branches that represent alternatives, nodes that represent decision points, and nodes that are probability event points. Admittedly, many of the inputs to such a model would have to be subjective evaluations; for example, the probability of achieving a given state of technology. The question of the value any type of subjective analysis may have may then be raised. Such analyses generally permit the following[20]:

1. The various parties to a decision to observe the basis for each other's conclusion.
2. The decision maker to draw on the intuitions and judgments of his staff without abdicating his decision making prerogative.
3. Sensitivity analyses to be made of variations in the estimates.

The use of a decision tree analysis could result in a preferred system, in terms of its figure of merit, being relegated to a decidedly secondary status. To make this discussion of system decision making and the cost-effectiveness criterion more meaningful, it is necessary at this point to describe in some detail the problems that may arise from the technological, resource, political, and psychological factors cited.

Technological Advances

Cost-effectiveness studies frequently involve the comparison of alternative systems with varying degrees of advancement in the state of an art. In such cases the crucial questions to be answered are, "will the specified state of the art advancements be achieved and when?" These answers become more and more uncertain as the state of the art requirements progress beyond the current technology.

Advances in the state of the art, moreover, may also provide collateral benefits; for example, in the field of avionics (aircraft electronics) great progress has been made in packing more and more performance into a given space or making the space smaller and smaller, while still maintaining the same performance, or both. The advent of solid-state technology in the electronics industry, of course, has been most responsible for making these and other changes possible. The point here is that state of the art advances can have both primal and collateral benefits that can affect system effectiveness and system cost, hence a system's over-all figure of merit.

Resource Availability

The development of a particular system may, in addition to the usual scarcity of financial resources, require such other scarce resources as

[20] *Ibid.*, p. 356.

highly skilled manpower, rare materials, or, as happens, all three. The economic problem, however, is still the same as stated originally in the introduction—that of allocating scarce resources among the competing factors for those resources to maximize the satisfaction obtainable from some set of agreed-on objectives. The point to be made here is that the resources to be allocated are not only financial but human and natural as well.

When the systems being analyzed are large-scale and would very likely be governmentally procured, it becomes desirable to examine the impact they may have on the resource structure of the national economy. One of the most significant measures of the size of any economy is the gross national product, which may be defined as, "the sum total of all the expenditures in a single year for all of the end products of the economy—consumer goods and services; goods and services purchased by federal, state, and local governments; new construction; business purchases of capital equipment; and net purchases by foreigners."[21]

The cited reference is an excellent source of data on the patterns of requirements and availability of resources in the United States from 1960 through the year 2000. Whenever the systems being analyzed are destined to be in competition with systems of other nationals (e.g., an antiballistic missile system), it becomes equally desirable to examine the effect they may have on the resource structure of such nationals. To illustrate the point, it may be generally stated that the Soviet Union's economy is roughly one-half the size of the U.S. economy, yet it effectively spends almost twice the percent that the United States does on its military posture.[22] On the basis of such a relationship it would appear that the marginal propensity of the Soviet Union to incur additional military expenditures would be roughly one-half that of the United States. Offsetting this relative disadvantage, however, is the fact that "the Soviet Union probably faces less severe political constraints" in making such adjustments.[23]

Political Sensitivity

Any decision making process can become quite unwieldy if the issues involved are in any way politically aligned. When the issues are complex system configurations and other selection criteria are involved as well, the selection problem can become overwhelming. Furthermore, there also

[21] Hans H. Landsberg, Leonard L. Fischman, and Joseph L. Fisher, *Resources in America's Future,* Johns Hopkins Press, Baltimore, 1963, p. 78.

[22] Charles J. Hitch and Roland N. McKean, *The Economics of Defense in the Nuclear Age,* Harvard University Press, 1963, pp. 84–101.

[23] *Ibid.,* p. 97.

appears to be a tendency for the larger and more complex systems to become more politically involved, since they generally affect more people and demand a greater amount or variety of resources. Several questions will be posed which serve to illustrate the kind of uncertainties that may confront a decision maker who is engaged in the selection of systems that are politically sensitive; for example: (a) how much integrity may the chiefs of state place in a military alliance; (b) what will the general public's reaction be to a department of defense proposal for deploying an intercontinental ballistic missile system on the nation's railroads or highways[24]; and (c) what will the action of a politically appointed governmental regulating agency be in approving a system procurement requested by a private public utility firm? Such questions are typical of the myriad of politically tainted situations in which the decision maker's efforts to make a rational decision can become the supreme test. A good intelligence-gathering system is really the only mechanism that will effectively mitigate the uncertainty surrounding the political criterion in any decision making process.

Psychological Stimulus

System developments may on occasion have a significant psychological impact, either planned or occurring by chance; for example, the German V-2 rockets of World War II not only weakened England physically but also affected the morale of the nation. These rocket systems carried with them an element of psychological warfare. Similarly, commercial systems may induce a psychological reaction; for example, in the design of automotive passenger cars over the years certain innovations by various producers have had a significant effect on shaping the over-all industry design trends for years afterward. Recall, for instance, the introduction of the fishtail style of rear fenders by the Cadillac Division of the General Motors Corporation in the model-year 1948.

The ultimate effectiveness of a system may well be founded on the kind of psychological reactions that may develop in its wake; for example, an orbital bombing system may be considered a rather provocative undertaking, hence may actually serve to generate the rapid development of effective countermeasures, thereby causing its effectiveness to be rapidly neutralized. In contrast, the same resources allocated to a less provocable bomber might not have stimulated any further countermeasure development. Similarly, in the commercial world a price cut by a small

[24] Such proposals have been studied in the interest of obtaining a higher degree of first-attack survivability by effectively denying to an aggressor any information on specific target locations, since the missiles would be at different locations at different times.

firm in an industry with relatively few producers sharing the market could be considered a rather provocative act by the other firms, thus inviting further price cuts in retaliation and perhaps eventually driving the small firm out of business. A less provocative promotional effort by the small firm might not have resulted in any reaction by the other firms in the industry.

Finally, the previously described figures of merit of a system may be shown to be a rather misleading decision criterion in comparison to measuring the system's merit in terms of its utility. Consider, for example, two equicostly military systems: System A affords only a 20 percent chance of penetrating the enemy's defenses but has a capability of destroying 75 percent of the enemy's retaliation capacity. In contrast, System B affords a 75 percent chance of penetrating the enemy's defenses but can only destroy 20 percent of the enemy's retaliation capacity. By using the conventional actuarial approach in evaluating these systems they would appear to have equal figures of merit of $0.15 = 0.2 \times 0.75 = 0.75 \times 0.2$. Further investigation, however, suggests the possibility that only a 20 percent loss in the enemy's retaliation capacity would be significantly destructive for our homeland targets, whereas a 75 percent loss in the enemy's retaliation capacity would not be *our* doom.[25] In effect, this is an attitude about these alternatives that is in part psychologically founded. The tradeoff of destructive capacity for penetration capability is upset by the psychologically haunting fact that the enemy cannot be assumed to be inflexible. A utility analysis would probably accord system A a significantly greater number of utils than system B.[26]

In summary, an introduction to the subject matter of system cost-effectiveness has been presented in four logical parts. Part I covered a broad range of those cost relationships of particular significance in system cost-effectiveness analyses. In addition, Part I provided a building-block type of background for Part II. Part II described the summation-type structure of cost models and their use in system cost-effectiveness analyses. It ended with an introduction to the concept of cost uncertainty and probability distributions of costs. Part III described system effectiveness models as being essentially a product series of fac-

[25] Assuming of course, that there is a limited range in target values because of the tendency for populations and industry to cluster in critical masses.

[26] The util is defined as one unit of utility, so that a higher number of utils for alternative A than for alternative B means that alternative A is preferred to alternative B. For an excellent review of utility theory see Chapter 22 in Baumol's *Economic Theory and Operations Analysis,* 2nd ed., Prentice-Hall, Englewood Cliffs, N.J., 1965.

torial deratings. It ended by introducing a method of obtaining the combinatorial product of the probability distribution functions of each of the independent variables involved. Part IV described various models for combining the system cost and effectiveness values obtained from Parts II and III, respectively. Part IV also discussed other factors that may be germane in the over-all decision making process. It ends now with a tripartite view of the system cost-effectiveness analysis:

Fundamentally the conduct of any professional discipline rests on a stool supported by the three legs of (a) the professionally trained and experienced practitioner, (b) the client, and (c) the problem.

The unfavorable reaction that occasionally befalls a systems cost-effectiveness analysis can often be traced to an inadequate consideration by the analyst of the other two legs to his effort, if not to his own technological deficiency. All too frequently at the beginning of a study analysts fail to probe the client in sufficient depth in regard to his purported problem, thereby failing to pursue any real problem that the client may have. In a similar vein, at the conclusion of a study analysts again do not spend sufficient time with the client to explain clearly what was done, how it was done, and what could be done further to aid the client in the over-all decision making process.

Ideally, the client's ultimate decision should be based on a judgment of all the pertinent criteria that he and the analyst can bring to bear on the problem. The analyst, in turn, will need to exercise considerable judgment in the implementation of whatever numerical methodology he may choose to use in the system cost-effectiveness analysis.

In conclusion, it is sincerely hoped that this discussion will help to develop a better understanding by both analyst and client of the comprehensiveness and usefulness of system cost-effectiveness analysis and to pinpoint its weaknesses and limitations.

SUGGESTED READINGS

- American Association of State Highway Officials. *Road User Benefit Analysis for Highway Improvement.* Washington: American Association of State Highway Officials, 1960. A manual on the relation of road user benefits to capital costs.
- Bellman, Richard. *Dynamic Programming.* Princeton University Press, Princeton, N.J., 1957. A classic text introducing the mathematical theory of multistage decision processes by one of the originators in the field.
- Crumlish, Joseph D. *Notes on the State-of-the-Art of Benefit-Cost Analysis as Related to Transportation Systems,* U.S. Department of Commerce (National Bureau of Standards Technical Note 294), November 1, 1966. A paper describing some of the problems and limitations of benefit-cost analyses.

- Enke, Stephen (Ed.). *Defense Management*. Prentice-Hall, Englewood Cliffs, N.J. 1966. A compendium of 24 authors on the operational analysis of Defense Department programs with particular emphasis on the managerial problems involved.
- Dantzig, G. B. *Linear Programming and Extensions*. Princeton University Press, Princeton, N.J., 1963. A classic text on linear, nonlinear, and integer programming by one of the pioneers in the field.
- Fox, Peter D. *A Theory of Cost-Effectiveness for Military Systems Analysis*. *J. ORSA,* **13,** 191–201, 1965. On a probabilistic approach to the measurement of cost and effectiveness.
- Goldman, Thomas A. (Ed.). *Cost-Effectiveness Analysis: New Approaches in Decision-Making*. Frederick A. Praeger, New York, 1967. A publication of the proceedings of a symposium on cost-effectiveness analysis sponsored by the Washington Operations Research Council.
- Hitch, Charles J. *Decision-Making for Defense*. University of California Press, Berkeley, 1965. An account of the Defense Department's organizational instrumentalities for allocating our resources in the task of survival with emphasis on the role of the cost-effectiveness analysis in the decision making process.
- Marglin, Stephen A. *Public Investment Criteria,* Studies in the Economic Development of India No. 4. The M.I.T. Press, Cambridge, Mass., 1967. A well-balanced account of the use of benefit-cost analysis in the planning of Indian economic growth recommended particularly for the advanced student.
- von Neumann, John, and O. Morgenstern. *Theory of Games and Economic Behavior,* 3rd ed. Princeton University Press, Princeton, N.J., 1953. The original and standard work on the concept of a strategy in the theory of games.

OTHER REFERENCES

INTRODUCTION

- Klarman, H. E. *The Economics of Health.* Columbia University Press, New York, 1965.
- *Transportation Science.* Published Quarterly by the Operations Research Society of America, Waverly Press, Baltimore.

PART I

- *Reviews of Data on Research and Development.* National Science Foundation Bulletin 41, Washington, D.C., 1963.
- Norden, Peter V. *On the Anatomy of Development Projects. IRE Trans. Engineering Management,* **EM-7,** No. 1. New York, 1960.
- Seiler, Robert E. *Improving the Effectiveness of Research and Development.* McGraw-Hill, New York, 1965.
- *Military Construction Pricing Guide.* AFP 88-16, Dept. of the Air Force, 1967.

PART II

- Feller, William. *An Introduction to Probability Theory and Its Applications.* Vol. II, Wiley, New York, 1966.
- Hahn, Gerald J., and Samuel S. Shapiro. *Statistical Models in Engineering.* Wiley, New York, 1967.

PART III

- Goldman, A. S., and T. B. Slattery. *Maintainability: A Major Element of System Effectiveness.* Wiley, New York, 1964.

PART IV

- Seiler, Karl. *A Cost-Effectiveness Comparison Involving a Tradeoff of Performance, Cost and Obtainability. J. ORSA,* **14,** 1966.
- Albert, Bernard S. *Cost-Effectiveness Evaluation for Mixes of Naval Air Weapons Systems. J. ORSA,* **11,** 1963.
- Archibald, Russell D., and Richard L. Villoria. *Network-Based Management Systems (PERT/CPM).* Wiley, New York, 1967.
- Landsberg, Hans H., Leonard L. Fischman, and Joseph L. Fisher. *Resources in America's Future.* Johns Hopkins Press, Baltimore, 1963.

INDEX

Antienergistic combinations, 79
Availability, continuous operation, 52
 cyclical operation, 52
 definition, 52, 53
 duty cycle, 53
 maintenance, 54
 multiple subsystems, 53
 prediction, accelerated environmental stress, 53
  mathematical simulation, 53, 54
 random operation, 52
 serviceability, 54

Beta distribution, 41
Breakeven point, 14, 15

Cash flow diagram, 33
Central limit theorem, 42
Coefficient of correlation, 19, 20
Conditional probability distributions, 42, 43
Confidence limits, definition, 47, 48
 degrees of freedom, 48
 estimated standard error, 48
 philosophy of integrity, 48
 t distribution, 48
Cost-effectiveness, contractual requirements, 1
 large scale versus simple system, 1
 military systems, 2
 other systems, 2
 system models, 71–102
Cost factors, geographic location, 20
 inheritance, 6, 7
 inputs, 9, 10
 level of use, 5, 6
 output, 10–16
 performance, 19, 20
 research and development, 7–9
 time, 16–19
Cost model aggregation, mathematical notation, 37, 38
 matrix format, 36, 37
Cost model expansion, coefficients of value added, 30
 machine computation, 28
 mathematical notation, 28–31
Cost of elements, mathematical summation, 27, 28
 statistical correlation, 25–27

Decision making and the cost-effectiveness criterion, political sensitivity, 98, 99
 psychological stimulus, 99, 100
 resource availability, 97, 98
 technological uncertainty, 97
Differential cost models, 38, 39
Discounted cost, 17, 18
Domain of feasibility, northwest corner, 72
 threshold filters, 72
Dominance, 76

Effectiveness model expansion, machine computation, 59
 mathematical forms, 60
 weighting factors, 59, 60
Error, 93

Fixed cost proration, error due to over-absorption, 34
 machine computation, 34
 sensitivity to quantity changes, 34

Geographic location, construction cost

multipliers, 20
Military Construction Pricing Guide, 20
standard domestic cost, 20
Gross national product, 98

Hardness (overpressure), 57
Heteroscedasticity, 26
Homogeneity, domain of feasibility, 72
geographic, 73
possession, 73
scalar, 73
time, 72, 73
Homoscedasticity, 26

Indifference curve model, antienergistic combinations, 79
combinations of two systems, 77–82
combinations of three and > three systems, 82, 83
constant cost curve, 79–81
constant marginal rate of substitution, 78, 79
diminishing marginal rate of substitution, 80
isocline, 82, 83
limitations, 83
nonsatiety, 77, 79
point of tangency, 81–83, 93, 94
synergistic combinations, 79
transitivity, 80
Inheritance, historical cost, 7
incremental cost, 6, 7
intangible, 7
"opportunity cost," 7
system cost-effectiveness, 7
tangible, 7
total system cost, 6
Inputs, capital, 9
factors of production, 9
labor, 9
market values, 9
material, 9
production function, 9
transformation, 9
Isocline, expansion path, 82
income consumption curve, 82
Isoclines, two-dimensional, 93, 94
three-dimensional, 94, 95

Lanchester equations, 58, 59
Least squares theory, 26, 27
Level of use, number of cost levels, 5, 6
ordering, 5, 6

Mathematical programming, calculus of variations, 83
dynamic, 83
integer, 83
linear, 83–86
corner solution, 86
feasibility boundary, 84–86
feasibility region, 84
objective function, 85
side conditions, 83, 84
nonlinear, 83
optimal control theory, 83
Mathematical summation, investment costs, 27, 28
operation costs, 28
R & D costs, 27
Matrix model, checklist, 23, 24
cost functions, 23–25
cost of elements, 25–28
grouping of elements, 24, 25
physical functions, 23–25
Maximizing total system effectiveness, calculus approach, 61–64
first order conditions, 61–63
limitations, 63, 64
second order conditions, 61–63
tradeoff approach, 61
Minimizing total system cost, calculus approach, 31
tradeoff approach, 31
Miss distance, 57
Monte Carlo simulation, 42, 43, 67

Normal distribution, 41, 42

Obtainability cost, 18, 19
Output, average fixed cost, 10, 12, 33, 34
average system cost, 10–13, 15, 16
average variable cost, 10–12
breakeven point, 14, 15
cumulative, 11, 12, 14, 15
first unit, 11
marginal system cost, 10–14
nonlinear average and marginal cost curves, 13
optimal efficiency versus optimal return,

13, 14
ratio of fixed to variable cost, 14, 15, 18, 34
relative activity of components, 14
short run versus long run cost, 15, 16
straight-line average and marginal cost curves, 12
total fixed cost, 10, 12, 14, 15, 33, 34
total system cost, 10–12, 14, 15
total variable cost, 10, 12, 14, 15
U-shaped average cost curves, 16

Performance, basic, definition, 47
CER (cost estimating relationship, 19, 27
cost regression, 19
coefficient of correlation, 19, 20
multiple parameters, catastrophic degradation, 49
graceful degradation, no redundancy, 49–51
graceful degradation with redundancy, 49–52
Period costing, definition, 31, 32
discounting analog, 32
natural life expectancy, 32
sensitivity analysis, 32
Period effectiveness, multimodal operation, sequentially, 65
simultaneously, 65
synergistic factor, 65, 66
single mode operation, 65
Period versus mission effectiveness, distinction, 64, 65
Planar graph, 75, 76
Population distribution, 47, 48, 67
Probabilistic cost, beta distribution, 41
central limit theorem, 42
conditional probability distributions, 42, 43
Monte Carlo simulation, 42, 43
degenerate cases, 41, 42
description, 39
matrices, 42
normal distribution, 41, 42
normalized, 41
rectangular distribution, 41
triangular distribution, 41–43
expected value, 41
variance, 41
versus fixed point cost, 39
Probabilistic cost-effectiveness, cost error, 93
description, 91
effectiveness error, 93
error combinations, 93
ratio model, 91–93
probability limit contours, 91, 92
two-dimensional indifference curve model, 93, 94
isocline paths, 93, 94
three-dimensional indifference curve model, 94, 95
isocline tube, 94, 95
Probabilistic effectiveness, description, 67
Monte Carlo simulation, 67
population distribution, 67
sample distribution, 67
versus single value effectiveness, 67
Probability of kill, single shot, 56, 57
Probability product model, basic versus realized design, 45, 46
equal parametric weighting, 46
over-all expression, 46
theory, 46
Professional requirements, 101

Ratio model, constant cost, 74, 75
constant effectiveness, 74, 75
definition, 74
dominance, 76
limitations, 76
planar graph, 75, 76
northwest versus southeast quadrant, 76
optimal efficiency versus optimal effectiveness, 76
variable cost and effectiveness, 74–76
vector solution, 76
Rectangular distribution, 41
Reliability, definition, 54
duty cycle, 54
graceful versus normal versus catastrophic degradation, 54, 55
maintained versus nonmaintained system, 55, 56
multiple mission, 54
redundancy allocation, 55
redundancy versus cost of equipment downtime, 55
Research and development, applied research, 7
basic research, 7

cycles, 8, 9
development, 7
prediction, 8, 9
state of the art advance, versus cost, 9
versus cost uncertainty, 9

Salvage value, 28–30, 32, 37, 38
Sample distribution, 47, 48, 67
Short run versus long run cost, 15, 16
Simulation, 53, 54
Statistical correlation, cost versus cost, 26
cost versus design, 25, 26
heteroscedastic, 26
homoscedastic, 26
least squares theory, horizontal displacement, 27
orthogonal displacement, 27
vertical displacement, 26
Survivability, commercial system, 56
definition, 56
hardness (overpressure), 57
macroanalysis, 58, 59
microanalysis, 57, 58
miss distance, 57
single shot kill probability, 56, 57
weapon system, 56
Synergistic combinations, 65, 66, 79
System, definition, 1

t Distribution, 48
Theory of games, description, 86
dynamic situations, 90
equilibrium versus nonequilibrium strategy, 87
game theoretic versus nongame theoretic opponent, 89, 90
maximin versus minimax strategy, 88
maximum strategy versus best strategy, 87–89
min-max solution, 87
nonconstant sum, 90
n persons, 90
payoff matrix, 87–90
pure versus mixed strategies, 90
relation to linear programming, 86, 87
strategy versus counterstrategy, 87–91
unstable game, 89
zero sum, two-person, 87
Time, charging for dispropensity to wait as a function of, 19
crediting for collateral benefits as a function of, 18
interest as a function of, 17
discounting, single sum, 17
discounting continuously, 17, 18
discounting serially, 17
negative interest as a function of, 18, 19
discounting, single sum, 18
discounting continuously, 18
discounting serially, 18
Time phasing cost, cash flow analog, 33
definition, 33
uses, 33
Time phasing effectiveness, definition, 66, 67
degenerative forces, 67
endogenous, 67
exogenous, 67
Triangular distribution, 41–43
Transitivity, 80

Utility analysis, 100

Variable cost nonlinearity, approximation, by linear segments, 34, 35
by cubic equation, 35, 36
Vector solution, 76